D0792180

"*False teeth* and a smoking mermaid"

Published by Age Concern England
1268 London Road
London SW16 4ER

First published 2004
Principal researchers and compilers Alex Grimaldi, Ben Marshall and Tim Southwell
Designed and typeset by Bob Searles
Production by GreenGate Publishing Services
Printed in Great Britain by Bell & Bain Ltd, Glasgow

A catalogue record for this book is available from the British Library

ISBN: 0-86242-391-0

"*False teeth* and a smoking mermaid"

Famous people reveal

the strange and beautiful

 truth about themselves

and their grandparents

In loving memory of Joan and Bill Alexander (Granny and Grandpa)

Contents

I know what my darling Grandmother meant to so many other people. She literally enriched their lives and she was the original life-enhancer, whether publicly or privately, whoever she was with. And, in many ways, she had become an institution in her own right; a presence in the nation and in other realms and territories beyond these shores.

At once indomitable, somehow timeless, able to span the generations; wise, loving, and an utterly irresistible mischievousness of spirit. An immensely strong character, combined with a unique natural grace, and an infectious optimism about life itself. Above all, she understood the British character and her heart belonged to this ancient land and its equally indomitable and humorous inhabitants, whom she served with panache, style and unswerving dignity for very nearly 80 years.

I know too what she meant to my whole family, particularly The Queen, to whom she was such a stalwart and sensitive support when my Grandfather died. For me, she meant everything and I had dreaded the moment of her passing along with, I know, countless others. Somehow, I never thought it would come. She seemed gloriously unstoppable and, since I was a child, I adored her.

Her houses were always filled with an atmosphere of fun, laughter and affection, and I learnt so much from her of immense value to my life. Apart from anything else, she wrote such sparklingly wonderful letters and her turn of phrase could be utterly memorable. Above all, she saw the funny side of life and we laughed until we cried – oh, how I miss her laugh and wonderful wisdom born of so much experience and an innate sensitivity to life.

She was quite simply the most magical Grandmother you could possibly have, and I was utterly devoted to her. Her departure left an irreplaceable chasm in countless lives but, thank God, we are all the richer for the sheer joy of her presence and everything she stood for.

Some of the wonderful cards and letters written by
Sir Henry Thornhill to his four grandchildren

EDWARD. WESTMOR.
WOOD
SIMLA. JULY
MY DEAR TEDDY.
I HAVE BE-
EN GO-
ING TO
LORD'S
CRICKET
GROUND
TO WATCH

WELLINGTON
GROSVENOR PLACE. S.W.1.

R WORCESTER
No. 15

Teddy E Ye Misses
Westmorland Wood
% Commander
A.W....

WELLINGTON CLUB.
GROSVENOR PLACE.
The girls c
home
first f
who C
Ms H
H

Misses Westmorland
Wood
A.S. Bemloe Simla
India.

"oh come unto those Yellow sands."

1914

Teddy takes his
Hathis for a walk.

Introduction

THE INSPIRATION for this book came from the world's largest collection of illustrated letters written by a grandfather.

Some years ago I discovered, in the back of an old wardrobe, a number of beautifully illustrated letters to my mother when she was a little girl. At first I did not know who they were from because they were all signed by someone called Kaka, a name with which I was unfamiliar. On enquiring I discovered that Kaka was my great-grandfather, Sir Henry Thornhill, and it became clear that these amazing letters, sent to each of his four grandchildren regularly for over ten years, were a unique expression of love by a grandfather. The drawings have been compared with the work of Beatrix Potter. Such was the interest in my discovery that some were published as *Pictures in the Post*, with a foreword by Her Royal Highness The Princess Royal.

Last year I was telling Ellen MacArthur about Kaka and she told me how special her grandmother was. I wondered whether other personalities like Ellen had special memories of grandparents. My son Alex was on a post-university gap year and, with his cousin Ben Marshall and another journalist friend, Tim Southwell, contacted personalities to find out.

This is the result – an enchanting and captivating testament to the wonder of the grandparent–grandchild relationship.

What makes this book unique and fascinating is that it clearly demonstrates just how universally special grandparents are. We are all of course the product of our upbringing, but the true extent of the influence of grandparents came as a real surprise. It has often shaped careers and helped others in crucial decisions through their lives.

"Kaka" (Sir Henry Thornhill) with Teddy

As you turn the pages you will go on a journey which taps into many private and intensely personal memories, often revealing a hitherto hidden dimension to the personalities and their backgrounds.

I would love to hear Tim Burgess, Stephen Merchant, Steve Pemberton and Ricky Gervais chewing over hilarious memories of their grandparents' false teeth ….

The late Bob Monkhouse's grandfather might have sprung straight out of the pages of Charles Dickens: white side-whiskered and hemispherically paunched, with rosy apple cheeks and twinkling blue eyes. Perhaps the fruit on his hospitable table came from the stall of Sir Michael Caine's costermonger grandfather, on the Tower Bridge Road. Sir Michael especially loved both his grandfathers, descended from the Irish gypsies, who came over to the Elephant and Castle. You can hear him saying affectionately of them in his endearing cockney accent: "Grandparents never get pissed off at you".

Until this book, I am sure that Katie Price and Paul Oakenfold were unaware that they share a common link to their grandparents. Paul blames his love of cooking, and his first job as a chef, directly on his Nan, and one wonders how much Katie Price's choice of career was inherited from her grandmother who was also a model – a topless mermaid on Hastings pier. Unfortunately, as you will discover, her career was beached. She was fired and left high and dry on being discovered smoking under water!

The extraordinary achievements of the climber Joe Simpson and the yachtswoman Ellen MacArthur stop you, as you reflect on the influence of their grandparents on their lives. Although Joe never knew his "Grandad Scotland", he says "I had always wanted to lead a life as exciting as his". Ellen's story is equally revealing, and the reader is left in no doubt as to where she inherited at least some of her incredible determination.

Despite the fact that Paul Weller never knew his grandparents, he speaks for so many when he says: "I think the relationship between grandchildren and grandparents is really important for society in general. One of the things I really wish for is not only to see my own children grow up, but to see their children grow up."

So you have already got the flavour of just some of the amazing and fascinating themes and traits of personalities and their lives which this book opens to the world, mostly for the first time. Above all, this book is a celebration of the special relationship that exists between grandparents and grandchildren; a relationship that transcends celebrity status, wealth, culture and religion; a relationship that is a gift to the whole world.

It is fitting that this introduction should come full circle to my very special great-grandfather, Kaka, who was the inspiration for this book, because the relationship which he achieved with his grandchildren against all the odds encapsulates the message from so many who helped to make this book possible.

These last words are from his grandson, my uncle Teddy, who hardly ever saw his grandfather, but who described him, when he himself was in his eighties, with a love that is echoed by so many of the wonderfully open and generous contributions from the personalities in this book:

"Grandfather Kaka was simply the best friend I ever had...."

Charles Grimaldi

Note:

In creating this book, Alex and I were determined that both the younger and older generations would benefit from any success which it might achieve. I chose Age Concern which is a charity that has a strong intergenerational initiative. This promotes all that can be so rewarding and special between grandparents and grandchildren, and indeed between the generations at any level – whether or not they are related by blood. I am, therefore, especially pleased not only that Age Concern is benefiting financially through publishing this book, but also that this book is intended to appeal to many people across different generations, a first for Age Concern's publishing operation.

Alex, for his part, and as the key to the very existence of this book, considered a range of children's charities and selected a little known, but very special charity – Railway Children. This organisation spends its limited resources trying to help the desperate plight of those children, some as young as five years old, who eke out their young lives on railway stations, abandoned and without any future except at the hands of those who seek to abuse them and take them into lives of prostitution and slavery. And so Railway Children will receive 10 per cent of the royalties accrued until the production costs have been covered, after which this will rise to 50 per cent of the royalties.

In this way, yet more money will be generated for both Age Concern and Railway Children to develop their work, enriching the lives of young and old, and helping at least some of the eleven million and more children around the world who have no homes other than the world's railway stations. Our intention is not only that both charities will benefit from this book but also that it will be a springboard for further recollections and will stimulate readers' special memories of their grandparents.

Shakira Akabusi

BEING BI-RACIAL I have two Grandads from very different backgrounds and very different worlds. I am lucky enough to know both of them and have been able to taste a bit of each of their lives. I feel that I have learnt some amazing lessons of diversity and culture from them.

Our travel begins as we step onto the crisp snow that awaits us at the exit of Düsseldorf Airport. As we leave our footsteps in the snow, like engraved marks on the walls of ancient tombs, I shall begin to talk about my Grandad on my mother's side. He lives in Warburg, Germany with Christel, his girlfriend of seventeen years. I love visiting him. When I do, I know that I will be in safe hands should anything go wrong. If I get ill, I know that I will be looked after by qualified doctors.

About a year ago my Grandad had a major heart attack but managed to pull through since he got the help and assistance that he needed. He was given a clean and average-sized bedroom to recuperate in after his operation and within three months he was able to return home to rest in the comfort of familiar surroundings.

The best part of going to visit my Grandad in Germany would have to be the food. I simply live for the breakfast. Lunch is never a let-down and dinner leaves me speechless. I just hope that when I grow up I will be able to cook as well for my family as Christel always does for hers. When I visit Germany, I feel so welcome and I am glad to have that experience in my life.

> **We found him in the grey, dusty and damp building that smelled like pee and rot. He was lying on the thinnest mattress with bugs and flies everywhere, his leg tied to the end of his bed so it wouldn't move.**

If you would like to join me now for a plane journey to a place further south and closer to the equator, I would like to tell you about my Grandad on my father's side. Our plane is skidding to a halt in Nigeria, West Africa. This story takes place in the south-west of Nigeria – Lagos. I found myself in a place I can't explain well. It was a place that, to me, looked like an abandoned building site, but I soon found out that it was in fact a hospital. Like my German Grandad, my Nigerian Grandad Daniel was very ill, only he had been in a car crash. We found him in the grey, dusty and damp building that smelled like pee and rot. He was lying on the thinnest mattress with bugs and flies everywhere, his leg tied to the end of his bed so it wouldn't move.

We just had to do something, so within hours we had moved him. It was an interesting trip for we only had two cars. We placed Daniel in the boot of the biggest car with my dad holding him and a chair to hold his leg and to keep him from falling out. I was in the car behind and saw how my dad tried with all his might to be strong. My Grandad, meanwhile, was in such pain. The painkillers given to him by the hospital did nothing so we gave him all we had. The hospital we took him to was not amazing, but it sure seemed like an improvement on the previous one.

Later that week we made a trip to my Grandad's village. The children there are so different to the ones I see in Germany. Small and undernourished with thin clothing, big bellies but also amazingly big smiles. Everyone in the village ran to my sister, my Mum, my Dad and me. Hugs all around and never running out of nice things to say about us and how glad they were we had finally come. Even though it was different to any place I have ever been, I felt welcomed and could see a part of me I wanted to know more about.

You may be wondering why I have not mentioned my grandmas through all of this. Unfortunately, they both died before I got a chance to get to know them. From what I have been told, they were both extraordinary women. I wish that I had met them but, since I cannot change the past, I am looking forward to reading about what other people have to say about their grandmas.

To sum up everything I have just explained, in Germany I feel at home and I know I am safe. In Nigeria I also feel at home but I do not know it half as much as I do in Germany. As I close I would like to make it clear that I am proud of both my Grandads and I am glad for everything each one has taught me.

Shakira Akabusi has shown promise as a young athlete and is also the daughter of athlete and television presenter Kriss Akabusi.

Leslie Ash

MY GRANDFATHER ran Lewis and Co, one of the biggest builders' merchants in the South, which he passed down to my father and uncle when he retired.

He was a very prudent man who, at an early age, taught me the value of money and how to save it. Probably due to him, I have always been very careful with money, some might even say tight!

Granny (Minnie) always had an enormous supply of sweets and cakes, and was especially fond of Fry's Chocolate Cream. Even though she died when I was four, I vividly remember her facial hair and aroma of ginger. When she kissed me on the cheek it would really tickle. I can still recall her whole face lighting up when she smiled. She was a beautiful woman.

> **" ... I vividly remember her facial hair and aroma of ginger. When she kissed me on the cheek it would really tickle. "**

The actress Leslie Ash is best known for her TV appearances in Men Behaving Badly *and* Where The Heart Is.

Nicholas Bailey

MY MATERNAL GRANDMOTHER, Marion Hippolyte, is a truly incredible individual. Even at 88, she is still a very dominant person, not in a forceful way but in a very gentle, loving manner.

We are very close, both geographically and emotionally. She lives just up the road from me in Birmingham. She was born in a small village called Fountain in Nevis and was one of four sisters. When she was old enough she moved to Turiso, where she met and married my grandfather, Jacob Hippolyte.

Jacob was from St Lucia. He died when I was three, but some of my earliest memories involve him. Friends and relations say he was a tall, very charismatic and well-educated man. At the age of twenty, after stowing himself away on a merchant ship, he became a naval chef. By spending a number of years in the merchant navy, he managed to see South America, the Far East and numerous other exotic locations. Due to his extensive travels, he became fluent in a number of languages including Spanish and French.

When World War II began, he was called up into the British navy. He served on a supply boat which was torpedoed. The experience left him slightly deaf in one ear.

When the war ended, he moved back to Turiso, where he met my grandmother. He then began a new career in an oil refinery. He didn't get on with his boss at the refinery, and after one particularly heated row, got sacked. Since all immigrants of Turiso had to have jobs in order to stay, the two of them, and their new baby (my mother), had to move away. They moved to St Kitts, where my uncle was born. Soon Jacob was moving again, this time to England. This move was due to his desire to lay down roots, and get a decent job in order to provide for his family. At the time Britain had a reputation as being a very prosperous place for West Indians to move to. This unfortunately was not the reality that my grandparents found. The reaction to their presence was at best toleration and at worst rejection. For educated people, who had fought for Britain in the war, this reaction came as a great shock, and insult, to them.

So my grandfather became stuck in England, performing a menial job and without any money to send to his family, or get himself back to St Kitts. His luck soon turned though, when he sparked up a good friendship with his priest, Paul Borrough. The young vicar of King's Norton near Birmingham decided to lend my grandfather enough money to get his family over to England. This level of generosity towards a West Indian was extraordinary at a time when boarding houses advertised themselves with the proviso "no Irish, blacks or dogs".

My father's parents, Kenneth and Cassie Bailey, loved each other very much. But after a few years of marriage, they simply felt they were wrong for each other. Therefore, when my father was still young, his dad left his family in Jamaica and emigrated to America. For this reason, my father and I have only just got to know him. In contrast, I knew my grandmother very well. She had a huge personality: a really strong, matriarchal, towering spirit. Outwardly she was completely different to Marion, but beneath the surface, she was just as kind and loving. While still in Jamaica she got remarried, to a man called Lambert Philpots. They moved to England when my father was fourteen.

I first met Kenneth Bailey in the late 1980s, and have been over to visit him in Kentucky many times since. He and his wife are very religious people, who proudly parade me and the rest of my family around their friends each time we are over. He was a trucker by trade, and

> " **This level of generosity towards a West Indian was extraordinary at a time when boarding houses advertised themselves with the proviso 'no Irish, blacks or dogs'.** "

has travelled most of America. He has nine children, so I now have a large number of aunts and uncles and a massive number of cousins. When he speaks he sounds just like James Brown. He has such a lot of confidence and joie de vivre.

I gained a number of character traits from my grandparents, one of which is the "devil-may-care", risk-taking instinct I have. More significantly though, I was given the belief that I could do whatever I wanted. I was always told that if I studied hard, kept my nose clean and focused on my dreams, they would all come true.

Nicholas Bailey's television appearances include over two years as Dr Anthony Trueman in EastEnders. *When not acting, he enjoys sport and ran the London Marathon in 2000.*

JG Ballard

I ONLY KNEW ONE set of grandparents. My father's parents died in the 1930s, while I was living in China.

When the war ended and I was released from the camp, I lived with my mother's parents for about two years in West Bromwich, while my mother and father were still in Shanghai. I disliked my mother's parents intensely. They seemed to me to be extremely limited in their outlook. They were very stuffy, very Victorian in their attitude – very negative. However some years later I was very surprised to learn from my mother that my somewhat starchy grandfather had been something of a maverick in his early days and had managed to outrage his straight-laced family by starting a band – he was a keen musician. It may be that some sort of wild artistic gene jumped from this strange old man to his grandson, me.

The problem with many of today's children is not that they don't have grandparents, but that they don't have parents. By contrast with my own relationship with my grandparents, I like to think that I have a very happy relationship with my four grandchildren. I hope that continues as long as I live. The oldest is six, and the youngest is three.

I think it is enormously important to have a large extended family. Parents, today especially, since both are probably working, cannot devote the kind of time to their children that they would like. And grandparents can step into the breach.

What do I do with my own grandchildren? Well, sadly, I am too old to climb trees and take them on adventure holidays, or ride rollercoasters, or play football. I wish I could. But I give them sweets and spoil them as much as I can.

James Ballard was born in Shanghai, to English parents, in 1930. He has written many novels, the most famous of which, Empire of the Sun, *is based on his experience of being interned in a Japanese prison camp during the Second World War.*

Lynda Bellingham

I REMEMBER GRANNY (my maternal grandmother Mab Carter) having wonderful, jet black hair (it never turned grey). She used to let me stroke and comb it. She was a very gentle woman, who would make meringues and cream on a Sunday afternoon, and would always have us sit in the conservatory to eat them.

She had a lovely, pretty doll ready for whichever granddaughter was coming to stay down in Worthing. We would adopt the doll for what was usually a fortnight's holiday, and with Granny's help, dress it up in fantastic little clothes. Grandpa (Charles Carter) was a very strict man, but, perhaps using my theatrical streak, I managed to win him over. He used to hide an egg somewhere in the house, and when I found it, Granny would cook it for my breakfast.

One of the clearest memories I have of Nanny and Grandpa's (Louise and Jim Bellingham's) farm near High Wycombe, was the bull that lived in a field close to their house. I would often watch it, and think how terribly ferocious it looked. Grandpa Bellingham was a man of few words who would always sit with his feet up, next to a roaring fire (summer or winter), holding a bag of sweets. The highlight of my stays with Nanny and Grandpa Bellingham was watching *Robin Hood* on a Sunday afternoon. Mum and Dad didn't entirely approve because they felt that it was rude to have the television on during a meal, but grandparents always let you get away with the odd thing that Mum and Dad probably wouldn't.

> **" ... it is particularly important for youngsters to have a relationship with their grandparents. They may then realise how wonderful older people can be. "**

I do think that the relationship that children have with their grandparents is particularly special. Going to visit my grandparents always felt like a holiday. Because they are one step removed, they don't have to tell you off. They can spoil you. And they often do, since they usually have more time on their hands than Mum and Dad. They do these rare but important things with you. For instance, my sons did boyish things like build fences with their grandfather.

I also think that in an increasingly ageist society, it is particularly important for youngsters to have a relationship with their grandparents. They may then realise how wonderful older people can be. And that they too will one day be old.

Although she has made numerous television appearances, for example in All Creatures Great and Small, Second Thoughts, *and* Midsomer Murders, *as well as regular stage work, Lynda's definitive role may be that of the "OXO Cube Mother".*

Harold (Dickie) Bird

AT THE AGE OF 71 YEARS, I cannot remember much about my grandparents. However, they were very hard-working folk who brought their families up to be good Christians. My mother and father were like their parents, good and honest parents who brought their children up to live a clean life and help others.

My grandfather was a coal miner, like my father. They were brought up the hard way – they had to work hard and fight for what they gained.

Born in Barnsley (where he still lives), Dickie Bird MBE played cricket for Yorkshire (with a top score of 181 not out) and then for Leicestershire before becoming a leading and highly respected Test Umpire.

Rabbi Lionel Blue

WHEN I WAS A KID, my grandmother used to wake me up at night and, together with other elderly ladies in black shawls, we visited houses where the man was unemployed, and used to put small bags of money through their letterbox.

This took place in the East End of London and was carried out at night so that the giver and receiver never met. As a result, I do not think of angels as fashion plates with wispy wings, but as solid, workworn old ladies wearing shoes with cuts in them to ease their bunions!

The money was given on Thursdays to help them celebrate the Sabbath, which came in on Friday nights.

It is a most deeply remembered religious reminiscence from my childhood.

> " I do not think of angels as fashion plates with wispy wings, but as solid, workworn old ladies wearing shoes with cuts in them to ease their bunions! "

Lionel Blue OBE is a Rabbi from the Reform tradition of Judaism. He is also a writer and broadcaster, and frequently delivers Radio Four's "Thought for the Day".

Cherie Booth

ONE OF THE MOST IMPORTANT THINGS to me about families is the way they link together the generations and allow one generation to pass on the family's shared history to the next.

That was certainly the case for me with my grandparents. I was brought up by my mother and my grandmother in Liverpool. For the first two years of my life, my grandma was my main carer as I stayed with my father's family in Liverpool, while my parents carried on with their repertory careers on the stage, visiting me regularly when they were not performing. After the birth of my sister, when I was two, I moved down to London to live with my parents. This lasted for a little under a year and then my mother, my sister and I all moved back up to Liverpool to live with my grandparents. We stayed there for the rest of our childhood.

We were a close family and my grandmother, Vera, who was 51 when I was born, was a larger than life matriarch throughout the extended family and indeed in our street. It was she who taught me the importance of family and our family history, and it was she who insisted that we be brought up as Catholics. When my grandfather broke his pelvis in a fall on a ship, she had to go to work as a cleaner to support the family, and I will never forget her tales of how badly she was treated by the people she worked for. She lived to see her first two great-grandchildren. Both she and her daughter, my aunt Audrey, died within months of each other, and then I found that I was pregnant with my third child. When she was born I knew that I had to call her Kathryn, which was a favourite name with both of them.

My paternal grandfather George was the main male figure in my life until his death of lung cancer when I was fourteen. He was a merchant seaman and when I was a child he would sail off for six weeks to Nigeria returning home for ten days and then going back to sea. Although he was the Chief Steward's writer he was "tea total" (strong tea with two teaspoons of condensed milk). His vice was smoking Capstan Senior Service untipped all his adult life. He played the piano and I have many happy memories of the extended family gathering around his piano while we all sang. He used to play "Thank Heaven for Little Girls" for my sister and me. I owe to him my extensive memory for the words of all the great popular songs of the era.

My maternal grandmother, Hannah, died in her thirties when my mother was fourteen, and she had to leave school and look after her own father and younger brother. It is from her that I get the dark hair and dark eyes which I have not passed on to any of my own children.

> **" I will never forget her tales of how badly she was treated by the people she worked for. "**

My maternal grandfather, Cyril, was a miner, and I can always remember being fascinated by the blue scars on his face and the way he splashed the water all over himself when he washed at the sink. He was a man of incredible energy and hard work. He was self-educated, wrote poetry and got an external degree from Nottingham University. He was a stalwart of the Salvation Army, playing the cornet in the band, a member of St John Ambulance and a football referee. Even after he retired from the mines, where he reached the position of shot-firer, he continued to work as a nightwatchman well into his seventies. He was also an active

> " ... he was 'tea total' (strong tea with two teaspoons of condensed milk). "

Labour Party member and was secretary of his local branch for years. He died in his eighties but was tremendously proud that Tony had become a Labour MP.

Cherie Booth QC is a leading barrister specialising in employment, discrimination and human rights law. She is the daughter of actor Tony Booth and the wife of the Prime Minister, the Rt Hon Tony Blair MP.

Sir Richard Branson

20th April 2004

Dear Alex

My Grandmother wrote to me when she was 99 to say that the last 10 years of her life were the best she'd had. Wouldn't it be lovely if we are all able to do that aged 99.

She and her husband lived life to its full. He dropped out when he was 30 and lived in a remote farm house in the depths of Devon. Living off the land, beehives, orchards, fish in the river at the bottom of the lane etc. My grandmother would never stop, she was a Wren in the war, she drove ambulances, she won ballroom dancing prizes and she was the oldest lady in the world to hit a hole-in-one in golf aged 91. She was an enormous believer that if you keep your body fit you have to use it, and therefore to have a conversation with her necessitated keeping up with her on a walk!

Kind regards

PS – My wife's grandfather on the other hand worked as a railway driver for 4 years and some of that seems to have rubbed off on the family.

Entrepreneur, creative thinker and founder of the Virgin empire, Sir Richard Branson is a shining example of success in the modern world.

Bill Buckley

BOTH OF MY GRANDFATHERS died before I was born, but I knew both of my grandmothers.

I knew Lily, my maternal grandmother best. She lived with my parents and me. She played a very important role in my early life. She was my on-tap playmate and babysitter. She had endless patience, she was kind and always up for fun. When I went to school at the age of five, I was already playing cards and draughts with her. It was a good way to learn adding up. By then she had taught me spelling and how to tell the time. In fact, because Gran gave me such a fantastic head start, I was very bored and rather naughty during my first year of school.

I remember going on holiday to the seaside with my parents and Gran. We were staying in a two-bedroom seaside cottage. Gran and I had to share a room. One night she told me to shut my eyes tightly while she got ready for bed. I, of course, did not do as she said, and ended up seeing a fascinating mass of layers, funny shapes and strange things that I didn't understand, all wobbling about before she got into bed.

She was a very good cook. In fact she had been in charge of the restaurant in a very large department store. She and Mum would do about half the cooking each. I think that grandmothers have to be good cooks. A grandmother who's a bad cook would be a cruel thing indeed! It just wouldn't be right.

I do think that children need either a grandparent in their life, or someone to fill the equivalent role. Parents and children need time apart in order to dilute tenseness, and be able to look at each other without the claustrophobic day-to-day interaction. Grandparents act as this important point between them. They are often the best people, due to their life experiences, to offer advice to both their children and grandchildren. They are a disinterested, but absolutely never uninterested, party.

Bill Buckley is a Radio DJ, currently presenting a daytime show on BBC Southern Counties Radio. He is also a regular pundit on the television channel BBC News 24, and was co-presenter of That's Life.

Julie Burchill

I KNEW ONLY ONE OF MY GRANDPARENTS, Eliza Burchill, who features in my novel 'Married Alive' as Liza Sharp, the scene-stealing, pig's-head-eating grandmother.

Eliza was relentlessly high-spirited. Though she had had an incredibly hard life, starting work in a factory aged twelve and being so poor during her marriage that she had to pawn her wedding ring every Monday, she chose only to recall the good bits. She didn't whine or moan about what went wrong in her life, anymore than I do. I find people who do so incredibly naff and risible. She was very tough and so am I. She was a hellraiser and I am too. She was extremely opinionated and eccentric, insisting that space travel had tipped the world off its axis (which she said was a real thing, like on a globe) and made the summers worse!

My Gran loved upsetting received opinion and often did so by wordplay. She once turned away a Catholic priest with the declaration that she had been "a prostitute" (meaning Protestant) all her life. She loved to upset my Mum and the other demure daughters-in-law by getting mileage out of the shocking word prostitute, and once told the doctor, after a fall, that she had been "prostitute" (meaning prostrate) "on the floor". She was a little more sophisticated than me, but I can definitely see the influence!

A journalist and writer, Julie Burchill is best known for her acerbic wit and her unwillingness to shrink from causing offence. Until recently, she wrote a regular column in The Observer Magazine *and now writes for* The Times Weekend Review.

Tim Burgess

HE WAS REALLY GOOD FUN, MY GRANDAD.

I was really upset when he died.

My Grandfather died from cancer through smoking.

My Grandad was in the navy.

He was The Boss. The Top Boy. The Man.

He had a two bedroom house in Bolton and seven kids.

He drove the funniest car – an Austin Hillman Imp.

He had a huge gap in his false teeth from smoking a pipe.

He had Brylcreemed hair like a teddy boy and it formed this huge knotted mass at the back of his head.

His armchair was made of leather.

He taught me fishing.

He taught me origami. Taught me how to make a swan out of a piece of paper.

I loved him so much ….

Tim Burgess is the lead singer of the internationally renowned band The Charlatans.

Sir Michael Caine

I DIDN'T KNOW EITHER OF MY GRANDMOTHERS, they died long before I was born. The women had a lot of children in those days and it was very tough on them.

My grandfathers lived until their nineties. I loved my grandfathers. Grandparents get all the good stuff without any of the responsibility. Grandparents never get pissed off at you. The moment anything goes wrong, mum and dad take over. They were both called Joseph – Joseph Burchill and Joseph Mickelwhite. They were real costermongers. They were Irish gypsies who came and settled in South London at the Elephant and Castle. There was a great horse repository and market, opposite the old Trocadero. A lot of the Irish gypsy tinkers were into horses and everything.

South London back then was like Sicily, it was very gangster-oriented and very family-oriented. It wasn't the Mafia but it was like that. The morality was the same. The moment you kissed a girl, two of her brothers came round with a shotgun and an engagement ring. Very much old school. My grandfather on my mother's side had a fruit stall on the Tower Bridge Road. He told me that Alfred Hitchcock's father had a fish stall there – I knew Alfred Hitchcock was from South London. My father's side was from Billingsgate.

They would have been very, very pleased about my knighthood. They would have seen it as an advancement. A reporter, a German fella actually, once said to me "I've read about you, you're always on about class so why did you accept the knighthood?"

I said, "Knighthoods aren't about class, it's about honour and I am a man of honour." Also it takes my class into the area of knighthoods. God knows I'm not the first working class person to get a knighthood but at least I'm one of them. I know that my grandparents would have been very, very proud.

> " Grandparents get all the good stuff without any of the responsibility. Grandparents never get pissed off at you. "

One of Britain's best known actors, Sir Michael Caine has made numerous films in both the UK and Hollywood. In the early days he was often cast as a lovable rogue but his later career shows his versatility.

Lee Chapman

I KNEW MY FATHER'S PARENTS PRETTY WELL. We used to go up to Birmingham every four or five weeks, and spend Sunday at their house.

On my mother's side, I know my grandmother (Margaret Plume) very well. Shortly after having her sixth child, my grandfather, her husband, died, so she was left to bring up the kids on her own. For this reason she has never had a lot, but once she was able to give to her grandchildren, she couldn't help but do it all the time. Even though she was poor, her generosity was boundless.

While we were growing up, the highlight of the year for my sister and me was spending five or six weeks over in Jersey with Granny. She would spoil us rotten with sweets, cakes, pocket money and trips down to the long sandy beaches.

One of the things I undoubtedly inherited from her is my dry and slightly wicked sense of humour. This has served me very well in the football dressing room. The more sarcastic a player is, the less likely they are to get ridiculed.

I really believe that having a strong relationship with grandparents is incredibly important. Firstly, when the chips are down, family will be the first to help. Secondly it's important to keep a level of continuity within a family. It helps to understand where one comes from and provides the opportunity to interact with other generations.

Having played football for over twenty years, Lee Chapman's career has seen him play for many teams, including Leeds United.

Charlotte Church

TOMORROW IS A LOVELY DAY ....

My Grandfather (or "Bampy" as we say in Wales) is a wise and humorous man, who is always full of the joy of life and invariably has exactly the right kind of advice for me whether things are going well, or not so well.

Bampy was a member of several rock and roll bands in the sixties and has seen the music business from the inside, so he understands the ups and downs of my professional life. One of his favourite sayings, which he administers as medicine to me whenever I am being pessimistic, is "tomorrow is a lovely day".

The singer with the "voice of an angel" first came to fame while still in her early teens.

Stephanie Cook

I WAS SO LUCKY to have known my great-grandparents.

My great-grandmother (Martha) was one of the most amazing people I have ever known and lived to be 98 years old. She actually died in her own home on her 98th birthday, which was also Christmas Day. I was eight years old at the time.

We would often go round to see my great-grandparents when we were staying with our grandparents in Oxford, and we would pick fruit from the trees or help in the garden. Whenever we used to go to visit my great-grandmother, she would have a wonderful selection of homemade jams and freshly baked bread. She used to bake special mini cottage loaves for me and my sister. She did all her own baking and I don't think she ever bought a loaf of bread in her life!

Apart from baking bread and making jam she used to do the most amazing needlework, and when my sister got married my grandmother gave her an amazing embroidered tablecloth that my great-grandmother had made. We discovered that she had done one for each of her grandchildren and her six great-grandchildren as well. I am looking forward to getting mine when I get married at some point!

My great-grandfather (Ted) outlived her and nearly made it to his hundredth birthday. She looked after him for many years and always put other people before herself. She was always cheerful and thrilled to see us and she loved having children around. Her family was the most important thing in her life.

She really was quite an incredible lady and a great inspiration to me. I believe that the more you put in to life, the more rewarding it becomes, and my great-grandmother taught me never to be afraid of hard work. If something is worth doing it is worth doing well, and I always try to do the best I can, just like my great-grandmother did.

Dr Stephanie Cook MBE was born in Scotland in 1972, and studied medicine at Oxford University. However, she is best known as the winner of the Olympic gold medal for the Modern Pentathlon in 2000.

4th December 2002

Alex Grimaldi Esq
Eastbourne
East Sussex

Dear Alex

I enclose a memory of my grandmother. I hope that will be all right.

"I had absolutely wonderful grandparents. I loved them all, but the one I knew best was my mother's mother who was extremely beautiful and married to a clergyman. She loved beautiful clothes and she loved beautiful clothes for her three beautiful daughters, so whenever the bank statement arrived at the Vicarage, she would faint to see how little money there was and then stick up the envelope and leave it to my grandfather to open and rush out and buy lots of clothes before he came back and told her she couldn't. She also loved reading novels and particularly the classics, Anthony Trollope and Dickens, and Charlotte Brontë and she read them all day but when she heard my grandfather coming through the front door, she would always have some sewing ready which she would sieze and appear to be mending socks as he came through the door with her novel shoved down the inside of the sofa. She tried very, very hard at parish work and used to take the Mother's Union prayer meetings. On one occasion my naughty mother and her sister, who must have been about eight and nine, added the dog's and cat's names to the prayer list, so the entire Mother's Union were exalted to pray at the end for Raggetty Bones and Mewkins, and my grandmother had great difficulty not laughing.

She was a dear, dear woman and I was very, very proud to have her as a grandmother."

Lots of love,

JILLY COOPER

Journalist and novelist, Jilly Cooper OBE is the author of numerous books including such favourites as Riders, Score *and* Polo.

Ronnie Corbett

I REALLY ONLY REMEMBER one of my grandparents.

I lost the other three before I arrived in this world, and my Dad's Dad remains the only one who conjures up vague memories for me.

Occasionally my Dad used to take me to visit his father at his home where he was looked after all his life by one of his daughters, who brought up two sons and looked after her father all at the same time. I just remember my grandfather always seated by the fire, and his being very well looked after, with his carpet slippers on and his pipe on the go – one of those pipes with the wee metallic cover on it. I can remember him cleaning it out, tapping it, scraping it, refilling it and smoking it. I would join them all for a sort of Scottish high tea, which I also remember quite clearly because it always contained the most wonderful high pan bread, as we call it up there; that is a sort of bread that has a crisp top and bottom, and a very flabby, uncooked outside – if you know what I mean.

Ronnie Corbett OBE, well-loved comedian and deliverer of monologues, has kept the British public entertained for decades, with the eponymous The Ronnie Corbett Show *and* The Two Ronnies, *with the* Frost Report *and* Sorry!, *among many other television, film and stage performances.*

Edwina Currie

MY GRANDPARENTS were remarkable people, though I only knew my maternal grandparents.

They all came from the Baltic areas in the early years of the twentieth century, from the countries we now know as Lithuania, Latvia, Estonia and Poland. They were Ashkenazi Jews, pious though not desperately so, not fanatics by any means.

They ended up in Liverpool because it was a stage on the long journey to America, and like a few others they got so far and ran out of money. But my mother's father was a special character. He was solid, squat and handsome, a highly intelligent man who by profession was a cabinetmaker; he worked in wood till he was over eighty and only took off a couple of days from work before he died at eighty-four. His name was Joseph Crystal; his wife was Annie and together they had ten children, of whom eight grew to adulthood. On arrival in England, he took himself to Pitman's College to learn English and had the most beautiful copperplate handwriting. He insisted that English (not Yiddish) be spoken at home.

The oldest boys were apprenticed as butchers, because, he said, "the butcher is the last to starve." And then there was enough money to send the younger children to college. So Uncle Jack went to Cambridge, and Auntie Ashke to Liverpool University, and Auntie Zena became a deputy headmistress – not bad for a working class immigrant family.

To me, as a small child, my grandfather was formidable and rather frightening; he kept a strap on the back of the kitchen door and would threaten us rascals with it, but I never saw it used, ever. He was tough, smart but kind. I hope I take after him, even a little ….

Formerly a Conservative Member of Parliament and Government Minister, Edwina Currie is now a full-time writer.

Bimal Krishna das

I BELIEVE THAT CHILDREN learn a great deal from their grandparents, often a lot more than from their parents.

This can often be because grandparents are less strict, so children may feel more at ease with them. Obviously a parent must provide a balance of discipline and affection, whereas a grandparent will show only affection.

The Hindu religion strongly encourages extended family interaction, not just with grandparents, but with all relations, no matter how distant. These relationships help to give support, not only to children, but also to their parents. They help support the stability of life.

My grandparents lived in Punjab in Northern India. I grew up in Delhi, which is very far away from Punjab. For this reason we only saw them two or three times per year. My cousins and I would all go together to see them. In fact my grandfather would take us on bullock-cart and tractor rides around the village. That used to be so much fun.

In the farming village where they lived, there were a large number of peacocks. Although they were quite friendly birds, the only person able to feed them was my grandmother. They really trusted her. They even let her stroke them. She took me close to them sometimes, but they were always rather apprehensive. I actually managed to feed them once or twice, but only because I was with my grandmother. She had such gentility.

Since the Hindu religion has no hierarchy, we approached the National Communications Secretary of the National Council for Hindu Temples to tell us about his grandparents. (The National Council for Hindu Temples is the umbrella organisation for all Hindu groups throughout Britain.)

Dame Judi Dench

A PARTICULAR MEMORY I have of my grandfather is his urging me to swim in Castle Howard lake without my water wings. He was a very good swimmer and was always encouraging us.

Another memory I have of him took place on the sands at Weymouth. He promised to give me 6d (not 6p!) if I could find a doll in the sands. He obviously never expected me to, because 6d was quite a lot of money – but I did!

One of the nation's most widely respected and popular actresses, Judi Dench is at heart a stage performer, but has also won recognition and gained coveted awards for her film work. She was made a Dame of the British Empire in 1988.

Jonathan Dimbleby

BOTH MY GRANDFATHERS died before I was born and my knowledge of them is only through what my parents told me and in fading sepia photographs. But I have a strong sense of their characters.

One was a newspaper proprietor and the other a barrister. They were friends before my parents met and were very active and prominent in the Methodist community. Both were committed Liberals (my father's father worked closely with Lloyd George as his press adviser) and both believed in the importance of hard work. Their credo was justice, tolerance and understanding – except of swearing and alcohol (they both signed the Pledge). Their nonconformist values strongly influenced my parents.

My grandmothers lived (and flourished) into their nineties. They were very different characters but played a central and supportive role in the lives of my parents. My mother's mother, Kathleen, married my grandfather when she was eighteen and he was in his forties (but no-one appeared to raise an eyebrow even when he told her father that he fell in love with her when she was a young teenager). She was an uncomplicated and practical woman, a wonderful cook from the Mrs Beeton school of fresh, nourishing food in large quantities, and she had a vast kitchen garden which she tended herself. She did not sign the Pledge and was happy to drink (in moderation, "a little sherry, my dear") and smoke (heavily) until her death at the age of ninety-six.

My father's mother, Gwen, was brought up in Bath, but fell in love with the theatre in an age when for a young woman to tread the boards was to court deep disapproval and gossip. Undeterred she joined a travelling theatre group, but was 'rescued' by her family and dispatched to Ireland as a governess. She survived this and returned to London where she took a flat in Shaftesbury Avenue, the very heart of 'theatreland'. She was a woman of great warmth and intelligence, always curious and relentlessly energetic. Just before her ninetieth birthday she drove herself from her flat in Richmond to the National Theatre to see *The Royal Hunt of The Sun* ("Quite magnificent, my dear") but complained, "You know, I tried to find somewhere to dine but you can't find anywhere that's open nowadays in the King's Road after eleven o'clock at night." She ascribed her good health to the fact that she took a cold bath every day of her life. One day when she was a mere ninety four, she fell asleep in the cold water and caught a chill. The doctor prescribed antibiotics but she was fatally allergic. Otherwise, I am sure she would have lived long enough to have received a Royal telegram.

What was it about these two women? They were devoted to their husbands and, so far as we could tell, utterly happy in marriage. They were always busy; they never complained; they were curious; they were sometimes quick to judge, but invariably slow to rebuke; they were never bored; they only talked about the past when pressed; and they lived every day as if life offered hope. Their optimism, kindness and humour meant that we always looked forward to a visit – which is, from the standpoint of a grandchild, perhaps the greatest testimony.

The Dimbleby family has a long and distinguished association with broadcasting and journalism. Jonathan has written a biography of His Royal Highness The Prince of Wales. He also presents Radio Four's Any Questions? *and has given his name to ITV's weekly political programme.*

Jonathan Edwards

THE ABIDING MEMORY I have of my grandparents is of visits to Blackpool!

My Mum's Mum and her second husband lived in an apartment overlooking the North Pier where my Grandpa owned a "Jokes and Magic" shop. They were relatively wealthy and, as my Dad was a vicar, we were relatively poor. So my Gran would always spoil us all.

The highlight was always an evening out to a lovely restaurant. We would enjoy the food but, even more, I looked forward to Grandpa Paul doing magic tricks for waiters. He also had a little device that he put in his mouth to produce bird songs, and it was hilarious to see other diners looking round perplexed, to see whether a bird was perched up in the corner somewhere!

> **"He also had a little device that he put in his mouth to produce bird songs, and it was hilarious to see other diners looking round perplexed ..."**

Olympic medallist Jonathan Edwards CBE first leapt to fame when he made the World Record for the Triple Jump in 1995. He is now a presenter for BBC's Songs of Praise.

Tracy Edwards

I ONLY EVER KNEW MY GRANDMOTHER on my mother's side and even though she died nearly thirty years ago I remember her as if I saw her yesterday.

The women in my family have always been strong-minded and my grandmother, who was Scottish, was a small but powerful person. She held the entire family together and, as I host Christmas day for my family every year, I find myself thinking of our Christmas days spent with her. She really was the glue that bonded us.

> **In today's fragmented family structure, grandparents are often the only common thread and are more important today than ever.**

My three-year-old daughter is extremely close to my mother. Although she will know only one grandparent, it is, ironically, her grandmother on her mother's side. I value their close relationship, and know how important it will be to my daughter to remember her grandmother as I remember mine.

In today's fragmented family structure, grandparents are often the only common thread and are more important today than ever.

Tracy Edwards MBE first made headlines as the skipper of the first all female crew in the 1989–90 Whitbread Round The World Race. Since then she has rarely been out of the record books.

Frederick Forsyth

I NEVER KNEW EITHER OF MY GRANDFATHERS, for both died in the forty months before I was born in 1938. Each died much too young, leaving my two grandmothers, who lived into their nineties, to remain widows for forty years.

Grandpa Forsyth had only shortly retired from a career in the navy to become steward of a working men's club, when a heart attack took him away, aged fifty-four. In the navy, he had been a Chief Petty Officer PT instructor for years and years, as well as the boxing, wrestling and bayonet-fighting champion of the Nore Command, which back then was huge.

He was quite muscle-bound, and had over-exercised himself to a cardiac arrest. I have spent much of life on a sun-lounger watching the joggers go by and avoiding the same mistake!

Grandpa Green died a year later, also in his mid-fifties, and also from "his heart, you know". He was a garage owner and a fanatical bowls player. One suspects missing the captaincy [of the bowls

> **They worked hard, saved hard, played gently, obeyed the law, paid due taxes, voted on principle, revered the Crown and praised their God. They survived two hideous wars and never flinched. People like that were the salt of the earth.**

team] might have provoked the heart. It was certainly not from throwing matelots half his age around.

Grandma Forsyth had been a housemaid when, aged twenty, she married her young able seaman, and produced three sons at five-year intervals. (Grandpa only came home once every five years!) The eldest was my father, but all three visited her regularly, with their own offspring, until she died.

> ❝ Grandma Forsyth had been a housemaid when, aged twenty, she married her young able seaman, and produced three sons at five-year intervals. (Grandpa only came home once every five years!) ❞

As a small boy, I thought sixty was incredibly ancient, never mind ninety, so I recall her always the same – snow-haired, gentle, always with a kettle on the hob for any visitor's cup of tea.

Grandma Green went on even longer. My mother was her eldest of three daughters, and she lived her widowed life away with Eunice, the youngest, who inherited the house in Gillingham, in exchange. So either Grandma visited us, driven by Aunt Eunice, for she never learned to drive, or we drove from Ashford to Gillingham.

She was from Lancashire, and her accent was pristine until the day she died. She introduced me to northern humour in the form of Albert Modley and Al Read. She had known poverty and the hard times; she was an inch short of five feet tall, fearless and indomitable. When she mentioned "the day the Queen died", she meant not Alexandra, nor yet Mary of Teck. She meant Victoria.

> ❝ As a small boy, I thought sixty was incredibly ancient, never mind ninety ... ❞

They worked hard, saved hard, played gently, obeyed the law, paid due taxes, voted on principle, revered the Crown and praised their God. They survived two hideous wars and never flinched. People like that were the salt of the earth.

Frederick Forsyth OBE was brought up in Ashford, Kent, and began his professional life as a reporter. In 1970, he began a successful career as a novelist, drawing upon his journalistic skills. His many books include The Day of the Jackal *and* The Odessa File.

Martin Freeman

UNFORTUNATELY, I never knew my grandparents well. My girlfriend's relationship with her grandparents is incredibly strong. Because I have never had first-hand experience of the relationship, I envy those who have.

I actually know quite a few people who are closer to their grandparents than their parents. They say that they can talk more easily to them. I've never really understood it. I can understand it mentally but not viscerally. I'd really love to understand it. It sounds so rich.

I think it's like that absentee father thing. They never have to tell you off so they get all the good stuff like taking you to McDonalds and buying you cool video games and stuff. When I see my two nieces playing with my parents, it is really lovely. On the one hand, the relationship between grandparents and grandchildren is very run-of-the-mill because we've been doing it for millions of years, but on the other hand it's very cosmic when you start thinking about where your life ends and another begins.

In the words of Paul Weller "As one life finishes, another one starts."

Born in 1971, Martin Freeman is probably best known at present for playing Tim in The Office. *Other recent appearances include Lord Shaftesbury in TV's* Charles II – The Power and The Passion. *He will play Arthur Dent in the forthcoming film of* The Hitchhiker's Guide to the Galaxy.

Ricky Gervais

IT IS A REALLY IMPORTANT RELATIONSHIP. I wish I'd known my grandparents better. I only knew one grandmother, and I love Gran and Grandad stories.

My Gran was a typical funny old lady, a bit grumpy, going slightly deaf, used to take snuff and send me money. She was that big matriarch figure. She died when I was about twelve.

I remember when I was a toddler, it would be "Let's go and see Granny!" and we'd go round to her house. It was one of those old houses that went to a basement and had four storeys but really small rooms. I'd go rushing in and shout "Granny!" As I was about to reach her she'd show me that

> " ... she'd show me that she'd taken her false teeth out. It was like an effect out of *The Matrix*, I'd go into super slow motion and do a complete 180 degree turn and then – wow – I was off like a shot. "

she'd taken her false teeth out. It was like an effect out of *The Matrix*, I'd go into super slow motion and do a complete hundred-and-eighty-degree turn and then – wow – I was off like a shot. Everybody would be laughing and I'd be this little white-haired toddler pinned to the ceiling in fear. Very, very funny.

When my mates start telling me about their grandads I'm cracking up, they're this route for everyone, a sort of common denominator of eccentricity. Grandparents are like this odd appendage, invariably they say something about you, but often in these oblique or exaggerated ways. Eventually, we start treating them like cartoon characters.

Without wishing to sound facetious it's very similar, in a way, to the importance of pets, because pets explain what death is when you're little. When you're six and your rabbit dies, you bury it and it never comes back and that prepares you for your grandparents dying. And that in turn prepares you for your parents going and then your parents going tells you that you're going to die as well.

When I was about six I was going to school and I said to my mum "How old will I be when you die?" And she said "Oh, you'll be very old," and I said "Will I care?" and she said "Well, you might be a bit upset."

I actually wanted her to say "No you won't be upset; when you hit forty you won't cry any more."

Ricky Gervais' career has included such diverse activities as working as a pizza delivery man, as a DJ for a London radio station, and managing a rock group. He found his niche, however, in the comedy The Office. *More recently, he has been seen in* The 11 O'Clock Show *and* Meet Ricky Gervais.

Rose Gray

THE HERBACEOUS SMELL IN AN ENGLISH GREENHOUSE REMINDS ME OF MY GRANDMOTHER IRIS, WHO WAS AN EXCEPTIONAL GARDENER.

Rose Gray is the co-founder of The River Café and author of several successful food and cookery books.

Susan Hampshire

Unfortunately I never met my grandparents, except one Granny when I was too young to really know. However, I feel having observed other grandparents, that they have a really important and wonderful contribution to make to their grandchildren's lives, and a lot of joy is exchanged all round.

With all best wishes, and hurrah for Grannies!

Susan Hampshire OBE has spent long periods on the nation's television screens – playing Fleur in the 1960s dramatisation of The Forsyte Saga, *and a decade and a half later playing Lady Glencora in* The Pallisers. *More recently, she has appeared regularly in* Monarch of the Glen.

Sir John Harvey-Jones

UNFORTUNATELY I hardly knew one grandfather, although the other I absolutely adored. My grandfather on my mother's side of the family was an inspiring man, although he had retired by the time I was born.

He had started by trying to follow a career in the navy, and when that failed he left for India to become an indigo planter. He was a very tall, imposing and gentle man who was interested in all the things which fitted him to become part of male society at that time – such as pig sticking, big game shooting, racing and all those sorts of pastimes. Strangely my grandmother never made quite the same impression on me, although she was a very strong-minded woman, who was killed when the Guards Chapel was bombed in the Second World War. She was absolutely tiny and ran the entire family with a rod of iron. She was a bon-viveur and pursued her pleasures and interests with a near fanatical focus. Amongst these were a strong liking for a little drink – and a near obsession with bridge!

Sadly I was never able to spend much time with either of my grandparents but certainly, albeit as a rather remote couple, they left a lasting indelible impression on me.

Britain's best-known business guru, and former Chairman of ICI, Sir John Harvey-Jones MBE is also known as the star of the BBC's Troubleshooter *series and the author of best-selling business books, and holds numerous prestigious positions on both national and international boards.*

Mary Anne Hobbs

MY FAVOURITE GRANDPARENT was my Mum's father William Penswick, an RAF pilot actively involved in World War II. His favourite meal was boiled tripe (sheep's stomach lining) and onions.

My Mum still tells stories of him coming home on leave from the war with as many pairs of nylon stockings as he could tie around his waist stashed under his uniform for my Grandma. (Nylons were a rare treat for any young lady and almost impossible to come by when Britain was living on rations alone.) He was a passionate man who would sweep my grandmother into his arms, lay her down and kiss her under the apple tree in the back garden.

He was so proud when I told him as a six-year-old child, that I'd been chosen to skate in the Junior Christmas Ice Show at Blackpool Ice Rink. He gave me 50p and six of his best oranges! My earliest memories are of a warm, wiry and wonderful old man who was already dying. Dying of a broken heart, after cancer cruelly took my Grandma away. Dying too of emphysema. His lungs were slowly filling with fluid, but John Players were his last pleasure, and he was damned if he was "gonna give 'em up", in spite of the fact that he was, literally, drowning. He was a heavy drinker, and would routinely need his car towing out of the ditch on a Sunday morning after a night on the sauce. I'll always remember a policeman coming to our house on the day he died, to tell my parents. I was eight years old, and the news crushed me. Even now, thirty years later, I can still remember his smell, the way that he laughed, and a warmth that would engulf me as a little girl. I will always miss him.

A highly accomplished music journalist, Mary Anne Hobbs is now a DJ and presenter of Radio One's The Rock Show.

Dear Alex,

Here is my quote re. my grandma:-

My fondest memory of my nan (Doris Ashworth) was sitting together in the afternoon with our eyes closed whilst she told stories of factory life, the war and her faith in God.

(Jane Horrocks)

Jane Horrocks is probably best known for her portrayal of "Bubble", Edina's dippy PA, in Absolutely Fabulous. However, she has played numerous other roles, both comic and serious, on stage and screen.

John Humphrys

I'm afraid I have no real memories of my grandparents – I've always regretted that.

I have become a father (again) in my late fifties and my relationship with my small son is quite different from the relationship I had with my other children 35 years ago. There's a sense of wonder about it that seemed not to exist when I was a young man. It's also possible (though very unlikely) that I'm a shade wiser now than I was the first time around!

Journalist, radio presenter and linchpin of BBC Radio Four's the Today *programme, John Humphrys pulls no punches when interviewing politicians or establishment figures.*

Tony Jardine

CATH, AS WE USED TO CALL HER, was a professional mother. She brought up four children almost single-handedly, while her husband (my Grandad Tommy) was away at sea.

Somewhere there is a picture of Granny Cath with her arm proudly linked through Tommy's sabre-holding hand, as he stands in full Naval Officer's uniform just prior to his departure back to sea, the big battle of Jutland awaiting the young lieutenant. She hardly saw him. Before World War II, he switched to the Merchant Navy. By then he was Chief Engineer.

He was once torpedoed on an Atlantic crossing but, as the lumbering merchantman's bows dropped in the heavy waves, the torpedo pierced the hull above the waterline and – without exploding – exited the hull on the other side, leaving two gaping holes.

Tommy organised himself and another engineer onto a bosun's chair as they laboured to weld plates in place to plug the holes in the freezing conditions. The thing he remembered most about the experience was the canteens of hot cocoa that were lowered over the side to them on a regular basis to keep them from turning to ice.

 On another occasion, Grandad Tommy proved to be very lucky too. He was to join a troop ship which was anchored just off the bar in the estuary of the River Mersey. As he was about to jump on one of the tenders to transport him out to his new ship, the air raid siren went off and they all took cover instead. One of the bombs, from a German bomber, managed to go down one of the funnels of the troop ship hitting the magazine below decks sinking the vessel within minutes, with a great loss of life.

Tommy survived the rest of the war to join the Cunard Line as a Chief Engineer until his retirement in the 1960s. While Tommy was enjoying his adventures, Cath ducked the bombs with her family during the Liverpool blitz of World War II, not knowing whether or when her husband would return. They must have been very difficult times.

Granny Cath never lacked energy or humour to tackle all her challenges. She would organise the family entertainment in the air raid shelter as if nothing was going on overhead – she made sure they all played their part. I can still remember her presiding over a big family Sunday lunch in the 1970s, where everyone was pressed into entertainment action including her with her own songs and very funny dances. Lunch lasted for hours and we all ached from laughter. But she couldn't get away from the sea. My mother eventually got a job in the Liver Building as a secretary where she met a young Flight Lieutenant from the Fleet Air Arm who was on short leave from Russian convoy duty where he was flying Swordfish biplanes from aircraft carriers.

Granny sewed his wings onto my mother's sweater, and at the end of the war the pilot sent my mother a boat ticket for South Africa where his Naval squadron was now based. And my Gran waved goodbye to her eighteen-year-old daughter with more water on her face than was in the dock at the time. She was used to great lapses of time from her loved ones, but three years later my mother was back on leave, heavily pregnant with me, and once I was launched so started the special link I had to both grandparents. They had a flat in Waterloo, Sefton overlooking the River Mersey underneath which was a small piece of beach where we made sandcastles and models of ships. So started my love of adventure and travel, stimulated by visions of great ships passing by and Grandad's tales of derring-do.

Most of all, I will be grateful to them for their support of our family in difficult times. There was trauma and tragedy in the family, and my mother ended up on her own working her way from humble cleaning jobs to being the administrator of a clinic. All the while, Tommy and Cath were there for us. When Tommy died an awful lingering death at home with Cath, we were all shocked. Whenever I called out for him his response would be "gone ashore". This time he really had gone and it took a long time to sink in.

Cath was strong and determined. Her resourcefulness was a lesson to me. She only went to the old people's home when she struggled to care for herself properly and of course refused our "port in a storm" at home. There she gained a new lease of life as the ringleader of a bunch of lively old ladies determined to enjoy their time together. When I came to visit, the nurses used to laugh out loud and say, "Your Cath has been at it again" – entertaining of course. At the time I was the pit-lane reporter on the BBC for the Grand Prix programme and it was at the height of the track wars between Damon Hill – the archetypal Englishman – and the very teutonic Michael Schumacher. The ladies always watched the Grand Prix programme because of me and Cath, but once they got hooked, they enjoyed the action. They loved Damon Hill and felt he was a gentleman who was succumbing to Schumacher's "dirty tricks". To the ladies, World War Three had started and Cath was at the centre of the action. She died in her sleep aged ninety-nine, to the distress of her new friends and her family.

Cath and I shared secrets and confidences like no other grandmother and grandson. Her advice was always spot on, and I miss her to this day.

The son of a Royal Naval pilot, Tony Jardine was born in South Africa, but returned to live in the UK in his teens. He became a rally driver and later a broadcaster. He now presents ITV's Formula One programme, but still regularly competes in rallies and circuit races.

Bruce Jones

I WAS VERY LUCKY to have two sets of wonderful grandparents: my English Gran and Grandad, and my Welsh set. I was very close to both of them.

I spent my childhood living mainly with my Gran in England, who looked after me while my mother went to work. She would give me my lunch when I left for school. I spent most of my time with her, and went everywhere with her.

She was with me when I needed her the most, a time of great worry for her when I was diagnosed with rheumatic fever and spent two years of my young days in hospital. She was there for me every single day.

My one promise to her was that I would be in *Coronation Street*! Sadly she died aged 88 and never saw this.

Bruce Jones plays Les Battersby in Coronation Street. *He has acted in many other productions including* The Full Monty.

Lorraine Kelly

MY GRANDMOTHER was a real character. Margaret McMahon used to squeeze every single drop of happiness out of every single day. She would wear expensive perfume to put the bins out and wash the stairs – she always said, "Don't keep things for 'best', every day is your best day!"

Lorraine Kelly was born and brought up in Scotland. She is now a popular presenter on GMTV.

Charles Kennedy

I HAVE VERY FOND MEMORIES of all of my grandparents, but it was my paternal grandfather who has had the most profound affect on my life.

I now live in the croft house that he himself built in the 1930s near Fort William in the Highlands of Scotland. I think about him almost very day when I am there. His presence is still very real. Much of the furniture that is there belonged to him, and the walls are adorned with photographs of him as a crofter and as an athlete, from when he fought in the First World War as a Lovat Scout.

> **" I now live in the croft house that he himself built in the 1930s near Fort William in the Highlands of Scotland. I think about him almost very day ... "**

My grandfather was widowed when I was only a young child and we lived in the neighbouring croft, which my parents still occupy today. Before I went to primary school, I was his almost constant companion on the croft, which is a small mixed farm. It was a magical upbringing with animals, and tractors to play on.

The Rt Hon Charles Kennedy MP is the Leader of the Liberal Democrat Party.

Glenys Kinnock

My grandparents were my friends. I was lucky that we lived close to each other and I could pop in for a chat, some sweets or just to moan about my parents!

We are grandparents now and it is the most joyous experience. It has also confirmed my memories of that special relationship you can have – when the time you spend together is so precious.

Glenys Kinnock has a distinguished political career and has been a Member of the European Parliament since 1994. She is married to Neil Kinnock.

Neil Kinnock

I ONLY KNEW THREE GRANDPARENTS – my father's father, Archie, and my mother's Mam and Dad, Sarah and Will Howells.

Archie was small, tough and stern – but with a twinkle. He was a great source of stories about his boyhood in the last decades of the nineteenth century and the great occasions when he saw Queen Victoria, General Kitchener and – best of all – Buffalo Bill Cody and his Wild West Show.

An ex-miner, a father of nine children – seven of whom survived into adulthood – and a treasury of Edwardian music hall songs, Archie Kinnock was (so my uncles and aunt told me) softer and sweeter with me than he ever was with his own children, or indeed anyone other than his wife.

My mother's Mam and Dad were very loving, terribly indulgent, and uproariously funny. Sarah was a marvellous cook with a strong personality, deep religious convictions, and a lovely singing voice. She went to chapel twice on Sundays and twice in the week ("to put in a word for Will" she said) and only went to the cinema – to see *The Sound of Music* – once in her whole life.

Will was – by contrast – a very irreligious, anything-for-a-laugh, lion of a man who savoured his pint. Like Archie he was also a former coal miner and he could grow any vegetable or flower, whittle wood into lovely shapes, and train a dog until it could almost talk. In addition, he was a devotee of cowboy films and he could get me onto the wooden seats of the Park Cinema for 7d before moving in the darkness to luxurious 11d seats in the balcony.

All of my grandparents were beloved friends who offered wisdom without solemnity, and helped to shape my values without ever preaching at me.

They knew poverty, war, industrial strife, unemployment, serious industrial injuries and illnesses. With some justification they could have spent much of their lives moaning. But they didn't. And it is their smiles and laughter that I still remember best.

In a different age, in a different world, with grandchildren of my own, I simply hope that I can give them joy that is up to the standards set by my own grandparents. I'm certainly trying – and I'm having a lovely time doing it.

> **"" All of my grandparents were beloved friends who offered wisdom without solemnity, and helped to shape my values without ever preaching at me. ""**

A former Leader of the Labour Party and former Leader of Her Majesty's Loyal Opposition, the Rt Hon Neil Kinnock has been a Commissioner of the European Commission for ten years, and will have been a Vice President of the Commission for five years when his term ends in October 2004.

Kathy Lette

MY MATERNAL GRANDMA was in her anecdotage, but from about the age of SIX. She bequeathed to my mother, and to me, a love of language, jokes and, yes, puns. My Grandma – crossword fiend, Scrabble champ, anagram-queen and walking thesaurus – was my favourite pun-pal.

A born storyteller, Mary Grieve lived for a hundred and one years. At the time of her death, her life had spanned almost half of Australia's European history. To her family she was a never-ending source of quality yarns about her adventurous past. Tales of bare-footed five-mile treks to bush schools which made us weep; encounters with snakes – both slithering and two-legged (they lost their dairy farm to debt collectors during the Depression which made us fume); raft trips up the shark-infested Georges River which made us nail-chew in terror. As an accomplished antic-collector, no doubt these tales were all highly embellished but they were also bum-numbingly entertaining. Young and old, we perched for hours at her feet.

She never read to us from books, but regaled her eight grandchildren with a wealth of stories. There were traditional tales, Aboriginal dreamtime mythology, folklore, legends, Bible stories, fairy stories – all told with a cackling sense of mischievous humour. ("Why are there no more fairy tales in the library?" I remember her chuckling to me, "because they ran out of elf space.") From the heroics of King Arthur and his Guinevere ("Arthur any more at home like you?") and the exploits of Sinbad the Sailor ("a crewed business") to Zeus sending Atlas off to hold up the world ("Atlas we are alone!"). From Eve eating the apple ("cores and effect, dear children") to the saga of her Norwegian father's shipwreck rounding Cape Horn, we kids sat, rapt.

It was obvious that my Grandma had grown up on a dairy as the woman could milk more pathos out of "The Little Match Girl" or drama from "Daniel in the Lion's Den" than any Shakespearean actor, "No holes Bard". (Actually, she didn't say that, but she should have. What can

> ('Why are there no more fairy tales in the library?' I remember her chuckling to me, 'because they ran out of elf space.')

I tell you? It's genetic.) My Grandma loved the English language and used it with grace and facility. She taught me the longest word in the dictionary – "antidisestablishmentarianism" – and the most useful word for an author – "lexiphanic" (given to the use of pretentious terminology, such as the word lexiphanic).

A schoolteacher by profession, she amazed her liberated granddaughters with the fact that, once married, she was forced to resign because the Married Teachers' Act forbade married women to teach. Years later when she had five young children, she was called back to service during World War II. After decades of permanent teaching, she continued as a supply teacher well into her seventies. At her retirement party, many of her ex-students, now retired themselves, turned up to thank her by creating a scholarship in her name.

Many virtues were reflected in her life: loyalty, honesty, duty, courage, kindness, compassion ("We all have our foibles", she once told me, "Aesop was famous for his"). But above all, she possessed a steadfast faith. Grandma was no wowser though, and at our many family gatherings she was always ready with a corny joke. She once asked, "What is pink and wrinkly and hangs out your grandfather's underpants?"

We teenagers, frozen with horror that such a risqué joke could emanate from our very proper Grandmother, could think of only one possible, blush-inducing answer. "Do you give up?" she twinkled. "Your GRANDMOTHER, of course!"

Mary Grieve, my beloved hundred-and-one-year-old Gran, a great storyteller, whose very best and most astounding story was her own. To conclude, I'm sure she wouldn't mind if, in her humorous honour, I told you that her jokes were like her Nordic eyes, blue as the sea, only cornea.

> " ... a great storyteller, whose very best and most astounding story was her own. "

Australian born Kathy Lette is well known for her wicked humour. Her bestselling novels include Altar Ego, Mad Cows *and* Dead Sexy.

Ellen MacArthur

I DON'T THINK I'M THE ONLY PERSON to have been inspired by their grandparents, and in fact I think many of us are, without realising it when we're young ....

My grandmother was always called "Nan" in our family. She was always someone very determined, though as a child I did not see that. Her story is one which proves this. Nan was born in Bradford into a poor family, and like all children went to school to get her education. Nan loved learning, and was a natural academic, this becoming evident when she won a scholarship to go on to grammar school. She was absolutely desperate to go; her passion was learning – it was the chance of her lifetime. However her father did not have the same ideas as she did, and forbade her from going as he needed her to go out and earn money for the family. Though bitterly disappointed, Nan went out to work and began working for a Building Society. During this time she got married to a fantastic man, and had three wonderful children – one of whom is my Mum.

Nan's dream of education was something she refused to let go of. It resulted in her taking several A-levels during night classes, writing her own poetry, and educating all three of her daughters at university. This was not achieved easily as her husband died young in his fifties, leaving Nan to support her entire family alone. She worked unbelievably hard, learning how to use computers at an age when most people would be thinking of retiring, and progressed in her job. When Nan did eventually retire, she moved into a cottage across the valley in Whatstandwell, just five minutes away in the car, so she was never far away from us and played a very active role in helping Mum look after us when we were kids. Nan came sailing with us on my Auntie's boat, and was often out for walks with me and my two brothers. By now she was well into her seventies, but Nan decided she would take her education a level higher! The first part of this was coming on the school bus every morning with us, and beginning to study a new language – German. In fact, she was in my brother's class!

She then went on to study A-level French and A-level German, which she completed in one year! Then, she decided to go on and study at Derby University.

She began a degree in European Languages, part of which involved a six-month placement in a university in Germany.

While she was in Germany, Nan fell very ill. She developed a mild form of pneumonia, which highlighted a problem with her lungs and meant she had a lot of difficulty in breathing. She was forced to take many months off from university due to her condition, and in time we realised this was not going to improve. Mum went to have a chat about Nan with the specialist at the hospital, and found he was aware of what Nan was trying to achieve. Mum was afraid that his recommendation would be that Nan could not go back, but actually it was just the opposite. I think he could see just how important the motivation was for her wellbeing.

When Nan completed her degree a year later, she was asked to give the speech at Derby University on Speech Day on behalf of all the university students for that year. She gave the most amazing speech, it was just incredible. I was always sad I couldn't be there because I was at sea, but I

> **'At the age of eighty-two, I went to Germany on a six-month exchange trip and I scored.' The whole place just completely fell about laughing.**

have a video of it, which I have watched many times. She had the whole audience completely in the palm of her hand, as she read from her handwritten notes. She talked about the fact that when she was young she had been unable to go to university, but that she always wanted to study. And then she said that people always asked her why she had waited until she was in her eighties to go to university – "Did she dilly-dally on the way?" This made everyone warm to her.

One of the lines, which I never forget, was: "At the age of eighty-two, I went to Germany on a six-month exchange trip and I scored." The whole place just completely fell about laughing. It was just beautiful. She paused, and waited until everyone had finished clapping. And then she said, "Because I was old, and in Germany that is respected." This made a big difference to her life in Germany – it was a fairly incredible thing to do, to spend six months in student halls of residence.

She died three months after giving that speech. It was a miracle she made it, but then again, maybe it wasn't … she was on a mission, she had a goal. She just never let that go.

She will always be a great inspiration to me.

Derby University offered me an honorary degree. I have been offered several honorary degrees but I decided that the one in Derby was the one –

because of Nan – so I took it. It was her wish that a foundation be started with some of her inheritance money to give a few hundred pounds each year to a student who had struggled through illness or financial pressure to complete their degree. I was there also to present the first of these awards. It was the first speech I've ever had to give where I couldn't actually finish it. I stood on the stage and I felt so strongly that I was in Nan's place that I was overcome by emotion, tears rolled down my cheeks as I choked to say my words.

Nan always encouraged us as children, and was responsible for me coming second in a writing competition at the age of six. When I decided to write my autobiography after the Vendée Globe, I found a letter that she wrote in 1996. I had completely forgotten about the letter, and found it as I was going through some old papers for the book. Back then I had been thinking about writing a book about the Round Britain Sail, which I was undertaking. I'd read other books that people had written about sailing and I was worried that my book wouldn't reach their standards, but she put in the letter, "Don't be stupid, of course you can." It was ironic that I'd found the letter at the time I was really struggling to write my book. She will always be there and, although it makes me feel emotional, I realised it isn't anything to be sad about – she would never have wanted that.

The other thing was that she left five thousand pounds to each of her grandchildren (three of us). Mum didn't tell us about it because we were all still quite young. When I tried to compete in my first big transatlantic race, we were desperately trying to find sponsors. We literally hit a brick wall because we couldn't afford to pay the entrance fee. When we didn't have a sponsor and it was just not happening, I rang Mum as an outlet for my frustration. She knew something was very wrong, and must have sensed how important it was. I hadn't rung to ask for financial help,

> **" " She will always be there and, although it makes me feel emotional ... it isn't anything to be sad about. " "**

but it was in that phone call that she told me about the five thousand pounds. That very day she transferred the money to France. Without that entrance fee being paid, we wouldn't have got the sponsorship from Kingfisher, because we wouldn't have been able to enter that race. So Nan is always there, supporting and encouraging me.

She really was a very special lady ....

Award-winning yachtswoman Ellen MacArthur MBE sailed alone around Britain at the age of eighteen, and six years later gained second place in the 2000 Vendée Globe round-the-world challenge. She is the author of Taking on the World.

Sally Magnusson

IN THE SUMMER OF 1930, when my father was eight months old, my grandfather Sigursteinn Magnússon brought his family from Iceland to Scotland. He had been sent by the Icelandic Co-operative Society to open a new office for fish exports at Leith, the port of Edinburgh.

He and my grandmother Ingibjörg stayed in Scotland for the rest of their lives, but fifty years later they remained as Icelandic as they were the day they arrived. Ingibjörg frequently spoke Icelandic when she thought she was speaking English, sliding happily from one language to the other and back again, often within a sentence. Even when she alighted steadfastly on English, her grasp was never completely secure, although no-one was much inclined to correct her. Who would not prefer to bring their school "chumps" home for tea? Or thrill at the prospect of the soldiers in Edinburgh Castle going on "gooard"? Or have the heart to explain why the grocer was baffled by her polite request for two "libs" of flour?

Traditional Icelandic feast-days were observed with exquisite cuisine and considerable panache, and none more so than Christmas Eve. In a development which astonished the neighbours, a glittering fir tree appeared in their window the first Christmas after the family arrived in Edinburgh. Presbyterian Scotland was not accustomed to pagan winter festivals, and the appearance of the tree, ablaze with candles in a window from which the curtains had been wantonly tied back so that everyone could see it from outside, caused a small sensation. Within a few years, Sigursteinn was happily boasting that people had started to copy him. I'm not sure he didn't come close to suggesting that he personally had introduced Christmas to the benighted Scots.

On Christmas Eve, at 6pm exactly, the family gathered in their finest clothes in the small lounge they called the "blue room", where Sigursteinn played his cherished gramophone record of an Icelandic choir singing the carol which defined their Icelandic Christmas, "Heims um ból", the hymn we know as "Still the Night". Then they would sit down to a dinner of thick rice soup mixed with cinnamon and sugar, dark ptarmigan with red cabbage, and frothy Danish pineapple mousse for dessert called fromasse, which melted in the mouth like foam. After the meal, Sigursteinn disappeared into the lounge, lit the candles, and revealed with a dramatic flourish the sight the children had been artfully denied since it arrived in the house the day before: the tree, candles flickering against the dark window, with presents heaped below. The family sidled around it, hand in hand, first one way and then another, singing carols until the last flame had died.

It was an evening which was later replicated in my own childhood and gave me a profound sense of belonging to a culture different from the one around me, and very special. My grandparents gave me Iceland – its language, its customs, and an ancestral connection to one of the most fascinating countries on earth. I'll always be grateful.

Like her father before her, Sally Magnusson is a television presenter. This extract has been adapted from her book Dreaming of Iceland: The Lure of a Family Legend, *reproduced by permission of Hodder & Stoughton Limited.*

Stephen Merchant

My paternal grandparents are, happily, still around. I see them as often as I can.

You won't find two more caring people. When you visit them, my grandmother constantly floats around you trying to ply you with cake and cups of tea, like one of those rug salesmen that you see hassling tourists in Cairo. Their names are Irene and John, though when they first met, my grandmother said her name was Joan. Apparently a friend had told her that you should never tell a suitor your real name. I'm not sure why exactly but I don't think my grandfather found out until their wedding day.

If I've inherited anything from them it's probably their cautious outlook. They're very cautious people. They always unplug everything before they go to bed in case there's an electrical storm and lightning shoots down through the wires and blows up the telly. They bought some plastic sheeting and duck tape recently so they can cover up their windows if al-Qaida launches a chemical attack in their area. My dad has assured them that the West Country is not top of Bin Laden's hit-list but they've got the supplies in just in case. It's odd, because from what I can tell my grandfather was recklessly heroic as a young man. During the Second World War he was in the RAF and volunteered for a stupidly dangerous mission dropping supplies. He only recently got his medals for his bravery, which he's justly proud of. Both of my grandparents have become more and more eccentric as the years go by, but I still adore them.

Stephen Merchant worked with Ricky Gervais at XFM, a London radio station, and continued the collaboration with the now internationally successful TV series The Office.

Bob Monkhouse

AT THE AGE OF NINE, my favourite person in the whole wild world was my paternal grandfather, Frederick John Monkhouse.

He was co-founder of the family business, Monkhouse and Glasscock Ltd, with factories in Hardwidge Street, Snows Field, London SE1 and at Devonshire Works, High Street Birmingham 12, churning out custard powder, jelly crystals, infants' and invalids' foods, cake and bun mixtures, blancmange and golden raising powders, soup preparations and celery salt, all under the banner of "Monk and Glass – At Last! At Last!"

Grandpa Monkhouse was a Charles Dickens character; white side-whiskered, rosy apple-cheeked, twinkling blue-eyed and hemispherically paunched. If I tell you that his laughter came in gales, that his rich baritone filled his great house like that of a born orator, that his readiness to like everyone he met was only exceeded by his unstinting love for children, then you will surely suppose that, if I am not wilfully exaggerating, my description may be distorted by the golden glow of nostalgia. As a young man, I wondered the same thing and so sought out older people who had known and worked with my grandfather. Their depiction of him tallied in every way with my own.

My great-grandfather was a ship owner in Cumberland and Frederick John was the youngest of his nine children. At the age of twenty-two, he came to London to seek his fortune, first joining a firm of tea importers and becoming manager. When his employers rejected his plans to reorganise their sales department by doubling the number of commercial travellers and giving them increasing commissions in reward for greater sales,

Grandpa joined a concern of mineral water manufacturers as a traveller. Here, he befriended S T Glasscock and told him his idea.

While visiting a wide range of grocers in the cause of taking orders for mineral water, the two young men also carried out a private investigation for themselves. In friendly conversation with each of the shop proprietors, they encouraged them to complain about inconsistent lines and seemingly attractive goods of unreliable quality. Within a few months they had compiled what they needed – a shortlist of products least trusted by retailers and their customers but nevertheless saleable.

"Somewhere on this list is our future," said my Grandpa. They crossed out a once famous glossy brand of toilet paper, a harsh scouring powder, and to Grandpa's amusement, the very tea imported by the company that had first employed him. They all represented entrenched competition and offered poor profits. But prominent among disappointing products were two fairly recent labour-savers: egg custard formula and ready-flavoured gelatine.

"Cooks and young wives have to spend hours making custard from fresh ingredients," my Grandpa reasoned. "Same thing with making jellies, boiling up gelatine, fruit juices, sugar and such. A really well-made custard powder which mixes up quickly and gives the same pleasing result every time is bound to succeed. Likewise, some kind of fruit jelly crystals. Let's make both under the same brand name."

They established their little factory in a tiny Bermondsey back street with only a handful of employees and invested most of their capital in development, paying high salaries to three talented research chemists.

Six months later, the partners agreed that they had exactly the right products and they hit the road once more as commercial travellers, this time in business for themselves alone. Within five years, their bright yellow label was a familiar sight on the shelves of thousands of groceries all over the world. Monk and Glass were now employing over one hundred and fifty factory workers and thirty travellers, all participating in profits. In the jelly business, my Grandpa told me, it's called "being set for life".

He married Miss Kate Jarvis of Faversham, destined to become the Grand Old Lady of my distant boyhood. I have a sepia photograph of her dressed in the manner of Queen Mary and sitting in a small open carriage drawn by two Shetland ponies, ready to tour her gardens in Forest Hill. She turns a cool and innocent gaze to the camera, as if jelly crystals wouldn't melt in her mouth.

Christmas at Terrington, my Grandpa's big house in Mayow Road, was a lavish, crowded well-fed riot. He sent chauffeured cars to fetch everyone so that the grown-ups could drive safely, arriving on Christmas Eve in time for hot toddy and oysters, in retrospect the oddest sort of appetiser but unquestioned at the time.

The twenty-foot tree in the hall was wired to the second floor balcony to support the profusion of its multicoloured load: stars and fairies and glittering balls of silver and gold, scarlet ribbons winding round pink cupids, crackers and candy canes, masks, ragdoll clowns and pierrots, all ablaze and cheery little lights. Heaped beneath it, solemn with promise, were a hundred mysterious parcels, one to be opened by each of the children whenever Grandpa drew his bos'n whistle from his waistcoat and blew it, a ceremony

> ❝ **The effect of his death on me was profound. I lost the ability to speak ...** ❞

that occurred at hourly intervals and had me and my nine cousins squealing and sprinting and tearing at paper with an energy that had the old chap crying with laughter.

The Christmas day banquet began at noon when Grandpa beat a three foot wide Chinese gong with a croquet mallet. His butler and two maids helped him to share out masses of food to us all: whole hams and turkeys with chestnut stuffing, suckling pigs, black puddings, veal pies, breaded sausages, great tongues with boats of Madeira sauce, and then mince pies and cream, rich dark cake, lemon tarts, brandy snaps, baked apples in cinnamon, rum babas, treacle pud and of course oceans of custard. Wines and spirits circulated freely and as the staff cleared away, everyone drifted into what Grandpa called "the convalescent club", a big withdrawing room full of comfy chairs. My Aunt Muriel and Bert Trouse would join the hired pianist at the Steinway to sing Victorian duets while the staff brought round China tea and liqueurs. Grandpa never served coffee – he said it made people testy. Then the adults dozed, the maids took the small children up to bed for a nap and we brats were wrapped up warmly and sent into the gardens to test the durability of our larger toys.

Once again, I feel I must reassure you about such idyllic memories. Those of my cousins who are still living have identical recollections of four such Christmases at Terrington. We also agree that none of us ever felt so well loved than as we sat on Grandpa's lap and looked into his eyes.

He was an extraordinary man, whose philanthropy was a byword. He was active in countless charities, a past Master of the Worshipful Company of Fletchers, a member of both the Livery of the Worshipful Company of Weavers and that of Needlemakers. Masonically he was past Officer of the Grand Lodge of England and also of the Grand Chapter of England. For those of his factory workers who needed such things, he bought bicycles, reading glasses and false teeth. When he died in April 1938, aged seventy-six, over two hundred mourners joined the family at the graveside in Norwood and the number of floral tributes was so great that three coaches were needed to convey them.

The effect of his death on me was profound. I lost the ability to speak and remained more or less silent for just over three months. It was possible for me to make a noise with my vocal chords but it was uncontrollable and unintelligible and it frightened me to hear myself. During my tenth birth-day party, I made a great effort to use my tongue and lips to produce a little speech of thanks but it was as if they were paralysed and I ran upstairs in tears. Schoolwork was difficult and unkind boys made fun of me. When I began to talk again, it was with a stutter that affected all words beginning with vowels. Even today, the same stammer can return if I am severely shocked.

It may be that most of us love because we need to do so, not because we find someone who deserves it. I believe that the devotion I felt for old Frederick John Monkhouse was so total and so enriching that, although it was very unlikely that I could ever have found someone else deserving such adoration, I continued to look for such a person, occasionally deluding myself into believing I had found them. So there was, in the first forty years of my life at least, a compulsion to love without reservation. It was a powerful legacy, Grandpa.

The comedian Bob Monkhouse OBE was one of Britain's best known entertainers. He died at the age of 75 in December 2003, after a courageous two-year battle with cancer, and is greatly missed. We are pleased and honoured to be able to publish his memories of his grandparents – perhaps they give us some inkling of where his talents came from.

Sir Patrick Moore

ONLY ONE *of my grandparents – my maternal grandmother – was alive when I was born. Her maiden name was Norrington, her married name, White. My grandfather – whom I never knew of course – was a barrister, and apparently a most delightful person.*

My grandmother too was delightful – and with a strong sense of humour. My mother always related one story about her; they were in Paris, in a hansom cab and the cab spring broke. Grandma (whose French was not brilliant) wanted to say "Coachman, coachman, the spring has broken." She managed "Couchon, couchon, le printemps au cassé."

She died in 1939, it was a sad moment. But at least she had eighty-four happy years.

Britain's celebrated astronomer, Sir Patrick Moore has written over sixty books on the subject. Since April 1957, he has presented every one of the monthly Sky at Night *programmes, for which feat he has gained a place in* The Guinness Book of Records *as the longest-serving television presenter.*

Sir Stirling Moss

As it is more than sixty years since my grandfather died, my memories of him are fairly cloudy. I remember him as a very warm and generous person who would give each of his grandsons a cheque for the number of years he had lived. In other words, when he was eighty, he gave each of us eighty pounds, and that was a great deal of money at that time! He had a small, grey goatee beard, and I remember him as being quite small yet with a warm persona.

A legend on the Formula One racing circuit, Stirling Moss received a knighthood from Her Majesty The Queen in 2000.

Cardinal Cormac Murphy-O'Connor

MY PARENTS, thinking that my home town (Reading) would be bombed during the war, left me over with my grandparents in the city of Cork and I lived with them for six months.

My grandmother was a loving but formidable figure and I think I was a little frightened of her. She wanted me to eat the crusts of bread for my breakfast every morning but I used to hide them behind a cupboard. All was well until spring-cleaning time and the damage was revealed! My grandfather was a wonderfully kind old man of regular habits. He always went out for a walk with his stick and his hat – and when he returned, he put his stick in the hall stand, his hat on the hat ring and went to sit in his favourite chair.

Come to think of it, a bishop is known by his hat (mitre), his stick (crozier) and his chair (cathedra). So perhaps some of my relationship with my grandparents paid off in my case: I hope kind, and not formidable, but with my own cathedral seat and shepherd's staff.

His Eminence Cardinal Cormac Murphy-O'Connor is currently head of the Roman Catholic Church in the United Kingdom, and is the Tenth Cardinal Archbishop of Westminster.

Paul Oakenfold

MY GRANDPARENTS, on both sides, were incredibly warm people. They often had big family gatherings at their houses. They were all very family-oriented people.

My father's father (Joseph Oakenfold) was a traveller and a gambler. He loved the horses. He would tell me all about the places he took people for his job as a travel rep. I particularly loved hearing about Spain. He would bring me pictures of matadors and bulls and make it sound like such an exciting and romantic country. Because of his experiences, I always wanted to travel myself. All my life, travelling has been one of my main passions. I put this down to him.

Joseph Oakenfold was an extraordinarily direct man. When I was fifteen, I took my girlfriend over to meet him. We sat down and after a long pause, he turned to her and said "I hope you're on the pill." This was hugely embarrassing, but he was the type of man who would just say what he wanted to say.

My mother's parents (Alice and Joseph) lived in Ashford, Kent. My Nan Alice was a chef and I would always hang around her in the kitchen. She cooked the most amazing roast dinners. When I left school, I didn't know what to do. I didn't have many qualifications but due to Nan, I loved cooking and knew quite a lot about it. So I can blame my love of cooking and my first job – as a chef – directly on Nan.

One of the saddest moments of my life was seeing Nan in hospital, shortly before she died. She was so ill I didn't even recognise her.

I know it's a cliché, but I really hope that when I have kids, I am able to explain how important families are, and that they should spend time with relations, especially grandparents.

Described by Rolling Stone *as "one of the founding fathers of the acid house scene", Paul Oakenfold is now a legendary DJ and music producer.*

Lord Owen

I CAN HEAR IT NOW, the tap of a stick against the wall as he walked down to the library, which was his study.

I was crouched in the corner almost holding my breath, waiting. He opened the door, closed it and, wearing dark glasses, walked over to his favourite chair. On the table was a large book the size of a big atlas of the world, although this was lighter and thicker. He leant over, picked it up, put it on his lap and began to turn the pages as if to find his place. I started to munch the boiled sweet in my mouth and the cracking noise was far louder in my ear than in the room. Then he bent down, took his slipper off and held it in his hand, his head cocked listening intently, then suddenly the slipper left his hand winging its way with unerring accuracy to my head. I ducked and it fell against the wall. Then we both began to laugh and I rushed over to his chair to give my grandfather Gear a big hug. I was only six.

I adored Gear. He was a most remarkable man. He had been blind ever since, as a boy of twelve, a pocketknife with which he had been playing slipped out of his hands and cut one of his eyes. He lost the sight of that eye in spite of all the care and skill with which he was treated, the other eye became infected and total blindness followed. His father searched high and low, and eventually found the only place in the country where blind students were prepared for university – at Powyke near Worcester. There, as far as possible, he lived the life of a normal schoolboy, playing cricket with a bell inside the ball so that the boys, though blind, could hit it and even catch it in the field. He became expert in Braille. The Bible in Braille occupied a whole wall in his library. I can almost smell it now, that big book with its thick brown pages on his knee. I would sit on the arm of the chair while he passed his delicate fingers lightly over the raised dots and read out one of his favourite passages, St Paul's letter to the Ephesians:

"Be strong in the Lord, and in the power of His might. Put on the whole armour of God, that ye may be able to stand against the wiles of the devil. For we wrestle not against flesh and blood, but against principalities, against the rulers of the darkness of this world, against spiritual wickedness in high places."

Gear taught me to read often from the editorials in *The Times*, listening carefully as I attempted to pronounce the difficult words and, when necessary, spelling them out. We would walk together down from his rectory to Llandow church, where he would read morning service and I would go to the village school. Living in Llandow I started to learn Welsh, and Gear, who spoke Welsh fluently and listened to the news on the radio in Welsh, would help me. It was an enchanting period. When I was fourteen, I read Siegfried Sassoon's *Memoirs of a Fox-Hunting Man*. I loved the passages describing the languid pace of country life because they evoked that time in the closing months of the Second World War in the beautiful vale of Glamorgan.

My father was away fighting the war and Gear became my substitute father, mentor and friend. For many years he cycled on a machine made from two bicycles bolted alongside each other. But I remember riding along the lanes on a crossbar of a single bicycle with him pedalling and me steering. My mother says this is fanciful nonsense. I retort that she was not there, having gone back to Plymouth to reclaim our house and to prepare for the war's end. But it does not matter whether it is fantasy or not, for this is how I saw our relationship. I was the eyes and he was the brain and the power.

A blind person develops a compensating hypersensitivity in all his other senses. In Gear's case his hearing was so sensitive that he could locate any noise, not just me munching sweets but cars a long way off in the country lanes. He walked those lanes by himself for many years, his stick tapping the road and swinging out to touch the hedges. He was never confined to the house and apart from his dark glasses and white stick, you would hardly have known he was blind. What fascinated me, as a child, was his consideration. On getting out of his pyjamas in the morning, he would always fold them neatly on the bed and reprimand me if I did not do so as well. He insisted on maintaining the acetylene gas plant, which made the gas for the lights in the rooms, all of which had to be individually lit every evening. He would always change the tyre on a car if there was a puncture while Granny Llew was driving. The blackout during the war was no problem for him since he knew where everything was in the house. He would collect the coal and firewood and light the fires. I still feel his influence on me. Rarely have I taken any important decision in my life before asking myself what he might have done in the same circumstances.

It was early in 1945 that I went to stay with Gear and Granny Llew at Llandow Rectory. My mother had been brought up there and I have a photograph of her sitting on an outside window-sill with her sister Aileen, and with Granny and Gear in deckchairs. Up to then, we had been living in Govilon, but my mother returned to Plymouth. So as not to disrupt her schooling my sister Susan, two and a half years older than I, stayed with a vicar's family at Llanfoist Rectory, very near the house in Govilon. The four months I spent alone with my grandfather and grandmother was one of the happiest periods of my life and the most formative. The Rectory was big and had a well-stocked orchard with lots of apple, plum and pear trees and a big loganberry bush by the door in the wall of the garden. I can recall the musty smell of the gaslights all over the house, even in the bathroom with its illustrated Mabel Lucie Atwell poem on the wall over the bath.

Bath nights in the glow of the gas were also story times. There, as Granny Llew read stories, and in particular poems, my imagination had me going to sea in a sieve in the land where the Jumblies lived. Or with the Pied Piper of Hamelin demanding "a thousand guilders! The mayor looked blue; so did the corporation too!"

Here I first discovered love for books and respect for learning. Gear was a wonderful teacher, feeling that knowledge was something vital to impart. After school at Powyke, he went to Jesus College, Oxford where he took his MA degree in history with honours. Then he went to the Welsh Methodist College. He was ordained a Methodist but the need to go on the circuit and move around frequently made it very difficult for him to learn the geography of each parish. Low Church and preferring simple services, he found it easy to transfer to the Anglican Church, becoming a curate at Gilfach Goch. Then he took the Jesus College living at Llandow, which later became part of the Welsh Disestablished Church. While at Llandow, he took further exams and became a Doctor of Laws, from Dublin University, where he was studying at the time of the Easter Uprising.

In church he conducted the whole service himself, reading the lessons as well as preaching, and people were amazed to find he could read with such ease and rapidity. He was also a good musician, playing the piano with some skill. He coached mature students for the universities and one of these, a local miner, went on to become the Bishop of Bath and Wells. He could find his way around his parish without assistance and apparently it was not uncommon for him to walk alone from Gilfach Goch to Ogmore Vale to visit his parents.

David Owen, now the Rt Hon the Lord Owen CH, originally trained as a doctor, but started his political life as a Labour MP (in Plymouth) in the mid 1960s. In 1981, he made headlines as one of the "Gang of Four", founders of the Social Democratic Party. He was elevated to the House of Lords in 1992. This piece first appeared in a slightly fuller form in Chapter 1 "Family" of his autobiography Time to Declare *(published by Michael Joseph 1991) and is included here with kind permission of Lord Owen.*

Steve Pemberton

I WAS VERY LUCKY in that I knew all four of my grandparents until well into my teens, and that we were very close.

Grandma Pemberton (Margaret) worked in a cotton mill, then as a school dinner lady. Grandad Pemberton (Jim) worked as a valve-tester for Philips, then as a caretaker for the GPO.

Grandma Catterall (Alice) worked in a paper mill, before opening a restaurant with my Grandad Catterall (Arthur), who was formerly a bookie.

They all lived in Blackburn all their lives. The four became good friends and would holiday together in Blackpool or the Isle of Man. This is how I thought all grandparents were – one big group, like in *Charlie and the Chocolate Factory*. Jim fought in World War II but was sent home early with stomach ulcers. Margaret, Alice and Arthur worked in munitions factories.

When my parents wanted to go away on holiday on their own, the four grandparents would come to look after me and my brothers. They were always exhausted by the end and vowed they'd never do it again as we were too much hard work. But they always came back the following year; Grandmas swilling the flags, Grandads watching the snooker with the sound turned up.

I inherited my dimple from Grandad Pemberton and have Grandad Catterall's hairline. Grandma Pemberton was calm and serene, Grandma Catterall silly and extrovert, and I think I inherited equal measures of each.

My brothers and I would put on plays at Christmas in which we would dress up as our grandparents and act out scenes of them all talking over one another. They loved it. They always took a lot of interest in my acting and were very encouraging. I remember playing Macduff's son in a production of Macbeth at Burnley Mechanicals. When it came to the scene where I was beaten and stabbed, I heard Grandma Catterall shouting "Eeh, give over!" They weren't big on Shakespeare, but loved it when my brothers and I recited Monty Python's *Four Yorkshiremen* sketch.

Grandad Catterall had a love of horror and would tell us stories about Dracula, then take us to see bats in the ruins of Blackburn cathedral. Grandad Pemberton would save his old caps, pipes and glasses for me to dress up in and encourage me to make up stories about the wickedness of my primary school teacher Miss Snape. Grandma Catterall would recite dirty jokes and limericks and pull funny faces with her false teeth. Grandma Pemberton loved to read and would give me Agatha Christie novels, as well as the inevitable knitted jumpers. I have so many happy memories of my grandparents and know that my brothers and cousins all adored them as much as I did.

Steve Pemberton was seen with Lenny Henry in the BBC Television series Lenny Goes to Town, *and more recently, co-wrote and performed in* The League of Gentlemen.

16 June 2003

Dear Alex,

"Granny Pratchett was very small, very intelligent, badly educated and rolled her own cigarettes. She carefully dismantled the dog-ends and kept them in an old tobacco tin from which she rolled future fags, occasionally topping it up with fresh tobacco. As a child this fascinated me, because you didn't need to be a mathematician to see that this meant there must have been some shreds of tobacco that she'd been smoking for decades, if not longer.

She spoke French, having gone off to be a ladies' maid in France before the First World War. She met Grandad Pratchett by chance, having taken part while she was there in a kind of pen-pal scheme for lonely Tommies at the front. I suppose it was a happy marriage – when you're a kid, grandparents just *are*. But I suspect it would have been a happier one for her if she'd married a man who enjoyed books, because they were her secret vice. She had one treasured shelf of them, all classics, but when I was around twelve I used to loan her my science-fiction books, which she read avidly.

Or so she said. You could never be quite sure with Granny. She was one of the brightest people I've met. In another time, with a different background, she would have run companies."

All the best

Terry Pratchett

Long before Harry Potter and Hogwarts were the Discworld *books, written by Terry Pratchett OBE. They continue to be widely read, and each new volume is eagerly awaited.*

Katie Price

MY GRAN *was a wonderful,*
beautiful woman. She was employed as
a topless mermaid on Hastings pier.

She performed behind
two sheets of glass which contained
water and bubbles. Men would
pay to watch her in her fish suit.

She was sacked for
smoking under water.

Formerly known as the glamour model Jordan,
Katie Price was born and brought up in East Sussex.

John Regis

*MY GRANDMOTHER is a special person
who, when I was young, would always go
that extra bit to make sure I was OK.
Always an adult's ear to confide in, when
my parents were too close for comfort.
I loved the sweets and cookies –
she was always a pleasure to visit.
She helped mould my way of thinking.
She taught me always to be true to myself
and try my best and be happy with that –
win, lose or draw.*

*London-born Olympic athlete and former world indoor 200 metre champion,
John Regis distinguished himself by winning six medals in 1990 alone.*

Marc Riley

OF ALL MY GRANDPARENTS the two that I became closest to were my grandmothers: both lovely women, both real "characters".

My Dad's Mum was a diminutive, hard working, constantly smiling lady who died when I was eight years old. I was devastated – this was the first time I'd experienced a death in the family, and the first time I saw my Dad cry. As a result most of my memories of grandparentage stem from my Gran from my Mum's side … Eileen Sinnott.

Eileen had retired by the time I came along in 1961 – though I know she worked for a Manchester-based company called Quiligotti's who made religious statues and iconography for the churches of the area. She was a painter and I believe that, to this day, many of the statues she worked on are still to be found casting an eye over the religious masses of Manchester.

My sister Tina and I spent many a Friday night with my Gran in the late sixties – we used to stay with her so my Mum and Dad could go out on the town without the expense of a surly fourteen-year-old babysitter. It was a much enjoyed stopover – more often than not we ended up all watching *Monty Python's Flying Circus* way past my bedtime. And if we were very lucky, my Uncle Chris would waltz in after midnight – with several bags of chips!

I remember the brilliant American comedian Lenny Bruce describing his grandparent's house as "having a strange smell – and newspapers with no 'funnies' (cartoons) in them". And I'd say that about sums it up. Not that hygiene was a problem … the odours used to come mainly from the kitchen where stews and ham-shank broths would regularly bubble on the stove – not a smell I encountered too often at home!

My fondest memories are of my Gran shouting at the TV – usually when a Labour MP was featured. She was one of the dying breed of folk who were staunchly Conservative and Royalist – despite not having that much to show for a life of hard work. Not rich – not poor I'd say. But she certainly hated the "lefties". I can't say her distrust of socialism is something that I've inherited. She also shouted at the TV the first time either of us saw David Bowie! *Lift Off with Ayesha* was the programme. Needless to say she wasn't impressed by the stick insect with spiky red hair and red leather boxing boots. Needless to say ... I was!

Another memory which refuses to budge is the time she tried to cut my hair ... without my prior knowledge! I was sat on the settee watching TV when all of a sudden – from out of nowhere – pounced my Gran with a tin bowl in one hand and a pair of blunt scissors in the other. She thought my trendy "feather-cut" was an eye-sore and literally tried to take matters into her own hands. I don't think I've ever moved so fast.

In the early eighties, as one woman came into my life, another left it. I married my wife Trace in 1982 – and my Gran died not long after.

My Gran was much loved and great company .... So, did I inherit any of her traits? Well I'd certainly like to think so!

Marc Riley (also known as Lard) co-hosted Radio One's Mark and Lard *show with Mark Radcliffe. This attracted one of the largest audiences in radio history.*

Angela Rippon

UNTIL I WAS SIX YEARS OLD WE LIVED IN MY grandmother's house in Plymouth. She had the two downstairs rooms; my parents and I lived upstairs. Cramped, but cosy.

Grandmother was ill for almost as long as I knew her, so her downstairs living room was dominated by a huge brass bedstead in the corner behind the door. It was from here, on bad days, that my grandmother "held court", propped up with feather pillows, lying snug and settled in a deep feather mattress.

She'd been born in Killiecrankie, and although my grandfather had brought her to Devon as a bride, she'd never lost her strong Scottish accent. So when I got home from school every afternoon, as I swung open the door to the tiny terraced house, I'd hear her call "Come away in ma wee hen".

> " ... as I swung open the door to the tiny terraced house, I'd hear her call 'Come away in ma wee hen'. "

No time to run down the flagstoned hall and up the stairs to see what Mum had for my tea. I'd push open the door to her sitting room, drop my schoolbag on the floor and bounce up onto the bed, drowning in the soft warmth of a thousand feathers, and snuggle into her outstretched arms.

When she was well, she'd take me to the Palace Theatre in Union Street, remembering the days when, as a girl, she'd run away from home in

Scotland to try her luck on the stage in London. She'd proved there really was a place called Killiecrankie (I never did believe it really!) by reading me a poem about a famous battle there. And she always took my side when I was cross or felt the weight of the world on my six-year-old shoulders.

One day she wasn't there when I got home from school, and the next time I saw her she was lying in a coffin in her best black dress, with white satin framing her plain, unadorned face, her long salt-and-pepper hair scraped back into her customary bun. I didn't cry, and I wasn't afraid to look at her. I was just very, very sad knowing that I had lost forever my best friend and confidante.

Angela Rippon OBE has had a varied career but is perhaps best known as breaking (with Anna Ford) the tradition of male only television newsreaders, and for presenting Come Dancing.

Lisa Rogers

I AM LUCKY enough to still know two of my grandparents – my paternal grandparents – and I knew my maternal grandma until last year when she died aged 92. I never knew my maternal grandad, as he died eight years before I was born.

Dad's Dad started life as a butcher before buying a farm with his brother and farming. Dad's Mum was a nurse in London, although she originally came from the same area as Grandad. Mum's parents farmed in Wales, after my grandfather had a mining accident, so he could no longer work in the Welsh mines.

As a nurse in London, Nana worked in St Mary's Hospital Paddington during the first part of the war. She tells stories about having to move all the patients down into the basement when the air raid sirens went off. But when part of the hospital was hit, the water pipes burst, raining scalding hot water down on the patients. It's really impressive that Nana did this, as it was virtually unheard of back then for women from farming backgrounds to decide to pursue their own careers, and then move to London to do so. I believe this attitude was instilled into her by my great-grandmother, Alice Huxley, who I can just remember. By all accounts she was a real character, and instilled a sense of self-belief and the importance of enjoying life into her children. My grandfather was in the Home Guard, as farmers had to stay at home and produce the food to feed the population. He says that "Dad's Army" really wasn't so far from the truth.

Both Mum's parents farmed during the war, and told stories of how the farm was accidentally bombed by the Germans who were looking for an allied weapons' store about five miles away. In spite of the damage caused, there was a certain smugness that the store was so well concealed that the Germans couldn't find it!

Lisa Rogers began her television career as a researcher. She is now better known on screen – as a presenter and actress.

Iqbal Sacranie

I CAN ONLY REMEMBER my maternal grandmother (Hoorbhai) because my grandfather died when I was very young and my paternal grandparents died before I was born. She was very important to me. She was very kind, caring and very concerned about my welfare. She had twelve children: five daughters and seven sons.

I often visited her during school holidays. In fact, when I was about fourteen I stayed with her for over a year while I went to school near where she lived in Malawi. In some ways she was more like a mother than a grandmother.

My grandmother was a very religious character. She valued the tenets of Islam. She practised Islam by performing regular prayers, fasting in the month of Ramadan, performed Hajj (pilgrimage) and gave regular charity. At eighty, she still practised her faith with great devotion.

> **" ... not only did she get me to pray, but she also made me see that the early morning is the best time to study. "**

She had great respect for my Dad, her son-in-law. She knew that my Dad was strict in many ways, and she tried to make sure that I was not too mischievous, and she paid attention to my education, since that was the reason I was staying with her. She also knew that a fourteen-year-old does not want to study and practise prayer, but she made sure that I did. I think the hardest part would have been waking me at 4.30 for the early morning prayers. By getting me up at this time, not only did she get me to pray, but she also made me see that the early morning is the best time to study. Your brain absorbs so well at that time.

At the time I may not have fully appreciated some of her actions, but looking back, I realise how caring she was.

One of the most important things that she taught me was to have humility in life. And that one gains more respect through character than through wealth.

She came from a rich background, but she still led a very simple life. She had great love and respect for the poor. When my grandfather was alive, the two of them would often look after very poor people. They would give them shelter and regular meals. If I were to be faced with such a task, I would find it difficult to accomplish. But she didn't. She really was an exceptional woman.

Iqbal AKM Sacranie OBE is Secretary General of The Muslim Council of Britain.

David Shepherd
O.B.E., F.R.S.A., F.R.G.S.

Granny went up and down like a yoyo and she had no idea what was happening. I was taking her out for a drive in her Austin 10. She was over 90 at the time, sitting on the back seat and we had a puncture. For a teenager with no muscle power, it was hard enough for me to get the car off the ground, exacerbated by the fact that Granny, a rather large, plump lady, refused to get out of the car; "Why am I going up and down" she queried.

She still enjoyed the drive and I don't think she ever discovered what a puncture meant!

The celebrated wildlife artist, best known for his paintings of herds of stampeding elephants, now lives in West Sussex.

Joe Simpson

MY PATERNAL GRANDFATHER, Grandad Jack, or Grandad Scotland as we called him, came from the village of Nairn, on the shore of the Moray Firth, not far from Inverness and in sight of the Monadhiliath Mountains. A little under a century after his birth I climbed on these mountains of his childhood.

To me Grandad Scotland was a heroic figure, a true Highlander who had joined the Black Watch regiment at the start of the First World War when he was only sixteen. At seventeen, he was wounded in the eye in the battle of the Somme, while fighting as a Lewis gunner. The doctor treating him guessed he was under age and sent him home. I suspect it was the compassion of a caring doctor for a young boy that got him Blighty and a discharge. The Blighty was the wound all soldiers dreamed of – serious enough to get home but not too serious, a bullet through the hand or foot, shrapnel in the legs, an eye wound, nothing too bad, just enough to get out of the carnage of the trenches and home to Blighty. A few months after his discharge he became old enough to rejoin his regiment legally, and fought on through the rest of the war on the Western Front, surviving the slaughter and reaching the dizzy heights of Lance Corporal.

> " **The Blighty was the wound all soldiers dreamed of – serious enough to get home but not too serious.** "

He told my Da that you could always tell which Highlanders had fought by the thick callouses on the backs of their knees. The heavy weighted hem of the battle kilt, thumping muddy and wet against the back of their knees, left a permanent war scar.

Between the wars Grandad Scotland served as an officer of the civil service in Jubbulpore in central India. He was commissioned into the Auxiliary Forces, and my Father (although he was born in Cheshire) spent much of his childhood in India, returning to boarding school in England, just as we were to do from Malaya, Gibraltar and Germany a generation later. I have an old sepia photograph of Da as a young boy, standing by a bird table with my grandmother beside him. She is beautiful and dressed in elegant 1920s style clothing. It is an image I could never reconcile with the frail and hypochondriac old woman I met on a few occasions in my later years. Draped across the bird table is a young tiger cub that had been brought in by a bearer after its mother had been killed in the jungle. In the photograph my father is feeding the tiger cub with milk from a bottle. It is like a glimpse into a fantasy world that existed only in fanciful books.

I have always treasured the stories passed on to us by my Da and the photograph of Grandad Scotland in India, sitting with his full-grown leopard Felix in his lap. He was a great one for shooting in the days when big game hunting wasn't frowned upon. He'd shot bear, deer, pig, peafowl, junglefowl, and the great delicacy, giant porcupine, but he had never shot a tiger. I had listened in awe to the story of Grandad Scotland's friend Harry Brewer, who one day, while in the jungle with gun bearers and porters, had surprised a tigress with its recently killed prey, a sambar, the largest of

Indian deer. The tigress had grabbed the deer's neck in its jaws and slung it effortlessly across its shoulders. Unable to retreat towards Harry and reluctant to abandon its kill, the tigress had approached a fifteen foot wide stream that blocked its escape. Harry, unprepared for the appearance of the tigress, wasn't armed with a sufficiently powerful rifle, and requested the gun bearer to give him the shotgun loaded with a single lead ball. Before it could be put into his hands the tiger had hurled the three hundred pound deer clear across the stream, leapt after it, grabbed it up and vanished into the jungle.

At the age of forty-two, after the outbreak of another World War in 1939, Grandad was mobilised as a reserve officer in the Cameron Highlanders. Too old for active service, he was first stationed near the Kyle of Lochalsh on the north-west coast of Scotland, guarding naval installations. Then, bored by such mundane duties, he took himself off in 1943 to British Somaliland, where he joined the Somaliland Camel Corps as a captain. He had one last adventure in the closing days of the war when he was involved in the capture of a German U-boat on the shores of the Red Sea. A camel-mounted Highlander leading his men into battle against the modern technology of the U-boat – pure Boys Own Paper!

I never met Grandad Scotland. He died of cancer a few years before I was born, yet he retains that reverential awe of my schooldays. Even today he seems like a figure from a Hemingway story, rather than a real grandfather. I had always wanted to lead a life as exciting as his.

Joe Simpson is a mountaineer and an author. His autobiographical book Storms of Silence *has recently been made into a successful film,* Touching the Void.

Ringo Starr

MY GRANDMOTHER was a big woman, Annie (I never called her Annie of course), and my Grandad was a little guy.

He'd maybe have a drink or whatever and get into things, and she would roll her sleeves up, clench her fists, take up a boxing pose and say, "Come on, Johnny! Don't talk to me like that – get over here, you little bastard." A big girl, she was, scrubbing steps and all, surviving. She was also the voodoo queen of Liverpool. If I was ever ill, my mother would wrap me up in a blanket and take me down to my Nan's, and she would fix me. She had two cures for everything: a bread poultice and a hot toddy – I loved those hot toddies! They were warm, and everyone would be fussing over me – the centre of attention.

> " He sat in his chair right through the war. He never went and hid anywhere, even though bricks were blowing out of his house ... "

Grandad loved the horses: "the gee-gees". He'd come in and, if the horses had lost, he'd be swearing and throwing the paper around – "those bastard nags, blah, blah …" just like any other gambler. Grandma would say, "Johnny, not in front of the child!" It was all pretty exciting for me. He had his chair which he always sat in. He sat in his chair right through the war. He never went and hid anywhere, even though bricks were blowing out of his house; he just sat in his chair. So as a kid I always wanted to sit in that chair. He'd come in, and he would only point and I'd have to move. But, of course, because it was his, it was the only thing I wanted.

Ringo Starr MBE was born Richard Starkey, in Liverpool. He taught himself to play the drums and performed in a number of local skiffle groups, before joining what is arguably the greatest band in history, The Beatles.

Chris Tarrant

My Grandad, Stanley Charles Tarrant, was the first person to teach me love for the countryside and, in particular, to teach me to fish. This has remained a great passion in my life.

He used to go for the most amazingly long walks and I seem to remember following him for mile after mile across the wild, open country of the Berkshire downs, with my little legs whirring along trying desperately to keep up with his great six-foot strides!

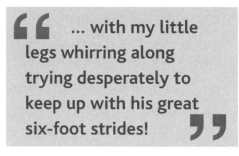

> **... with my little legs whirring along trying desperately to keep up with his great six-foot strides!**

He was always my best friend when I was a little boy and when he finally died at the age of ninety-six, it was one of the saddest days of my life. I still think about him a lot now, even though it's been more than ten years since we lost him.

I think the greatest sadness was that, although I'd had three daughters of my own by then, he had always wanted me to have a son and Toby was born just a matter of weeks after Grandad died, so he never knew. Toby was christened Toby Charles in his memory.

Chris Tarrant has worked in radio and television, presenting (among other shows) Tarrant on TV, Who Wants to Be a Millionaire? *and Capital FM's* Breakfast Show.

Lord Taylor of Warwick

UNFORTUNATELY I did not know my grandparents. This is a great pity, because I feel the grandparent-grandchild relationship is an important and special one.

The grandparent will normally have more time to talk to, and share experiences, with a grandchild than the parents have. The grandparent is also in the happy position of knowing that he or she can hand a grandchild back to the parents when playtime is over.

> " I feel the grandparent-grandchild relationship is an important and special one. "

I feel that the main attributes of a good grandparent are: a loving nature, patience, the ability to tell wonderful stories, and the possession of a packet of sugar-free sweets!

John Taylor was born in Birmingham in 1952. He qualified as a barrister, subsequently going into politics. In 1996, he was created Lord Taylor of Warwick, becoming one of the youngest members of the House of Lords, as well as one of the very few black and ethnic minority peers in the Lords.

Dennis Taylor

My Grandad worked in England and used to say "always buy expensive shoes as they last four times longer and look better than cheap ones."

My Grandma taught me to write and when I entered writing competitions I always got ten out of ten. Little did I know, as a five- or six-year-old, that it would one day stand me in good stead for signing autographs!

Born in 1949, Dennis Taylor is a sporting legend both in his home country of Ireland and around the snooker world. He has been a professional snooker player for nearly a quarter of a century, winning the World Title in 1985 in an unforgettable match against Steve Davis.

Margaret Thatcher

MEMORIES OF MY GRANDPARENTS

Both of my grandfathers died before I was born so my early memories revolved around my grandmothers, and most particularly Grandmother Stephenson who lived with us till I was ten. She was a stately lady and a forceful presence in the household. As a widow, she followed the custom of those days by wearing a long black sateen beaded dress, and for a very young girl this could appear somewhat forbidding. She had a strong sense of what was right and proper, and was a great believer in tradition. But she also filled the house with her warmth and her love, and was forever telling me and my sister Muriel tales of her own childhood.

Grandmother Roberts lived in Northamptonshire but rarely left her home, so I only saw her when we visited for holidays. These were always great fun as she never seemed to stay still for long, always bustling around her house and her wonderful garden, and sneaking small treats to Muriel and me. And though I knew her less well than Grandmother Stephenson, both were greatly missed when they were no longer with us.

The Rt Hon Baroness Thatcher LG OM FRS studied chemistry at Oxford University, but then went into politics. After several ministerial appointments, she succeeded Edward Heath (now the Rt Hon Sir Edward Heath) as Leader of the Conservative Party. In 1979, she became Britain's first woman Prime Minister, and continued to hold that office until 1990.

Alan Titchmarsh

MUM'S MUM, Catherine Naylor, came from Bradford, and her dad, George Herbert Hardisty, from Skipton. Herbert was a "ganger" – a sort of foreman – in the council's highways department.

He smoked a pipe filled with rich-smelling Condor tobacco and was bald with a walrus moustache. He seemed always to be wearing dark trousers, a dark waistcoat with a watch-chain, and a white collarless shirt. A flat cap (or black trilby on Sundays) covered the bald head when he was out. By the time I came along, he was retired and had time to be a small child's perfect grandfather, kindly and gentle with a few tricks up his sleeve.

While Grandad was short and stocky, Grandma was angular and slender-featured with swollen rheumatic knuckles. Of our two grandmothers, she was the one who spoiled my sister and me the most.

In the back kitchen of the Hardisty household in Ash Grove – the other side of the Leeds Road from Dean Street and where we would visit them two or three times a week – were produced toasted currant teacakes, spread with butter that melted and ran in rivulets down our chins. Grandma had an amber sugarbowl, and Grandpa would keep his empty tobacco tins and matchboxes for us, making long trains out of them and pushing them over the edge of the brown chenille-covered table to land with a clatter on the stone-flagged floor. He could make a squeaking noise with his hands – we called it "cupty-cupty" – and, to the despair of my mother, he would drink his tea from his saucer, having poured it there from his cup to cool it down before slurping it up under the drooping grey whiskers of his moustache. Then he'd wink at us, fill his pipe and sit by the open fire to smoke it.

Sometimes, in moments of sentimentality, he would sing "My Old Dutch" to Grandma, who would turn away and mutter, "Shut up, Herbert," wiping a tear from her eye with the corner of her pinny.

> " ... to the despair of my mother, he would drink his tea from his saucer, having poured it there from his cup to cool it down before slurping it up under the drooping grey whiskers of his moustache. "

The nation's favourite gardener, Alan Titchmarsh MBE found his way into every living room with the BBC's Ground Force *team. He has now reaped a second crop of success as a novelist.*

Denise Van Outen

THE CRUCIAL EVENT of the past year was my grandmother being diagnosed with breast and skin cancer.

She ignored a lump on her breast, believing it would go away if she applied Vaseline. My Mum said, "How long have you had this?" and she said, "Three years." At the age of eighty, she has refused chemotherapy – a decision I totally understand.

When my Grandad died, my Nan joined a pensioners' club and was out every night. She came home one day and said, "I've been on a date." This was about four years ago. She had a fantastic time – he took her out in his three-wheeler. For weeks she'd be saying, "What shall I wear for our next date?" she had this glow of being in love. They married in a big, raucous Essex wedding, and we tied tin cans to the three-wheeler.

So when my Nan does eventually pass away, I'll be heartbroken, but also very proud to know that she had such a great life.

Denise Van Outen first found fame as a presenter of Channel Four's The Big Breakfast. *Her career since then has included more television, films and a spell in the stage version of the musical* Chicago. *This excerpt is from an interview published in December 2003, and is reproduced with kind permission of* You Magazine.

Jeremy Vine

MY GRANDMOTHER, Rosamond, died several years ago but was wonderful. She pronounced golf as "goff" and would always come back from holidays and say: "Oh, the whole trip was a DISASTER!" For whatever reason: the weather, the travel, anything. It was against her religion to enjoy a holiday. She was visiting elderly people into her late eighties, at a point where some of them were younger than her.

Award-winning broadcaster and journalist, Jeremy Vine was born in 1965. He now appears regularly on Newsnight *and since 2003 has presented* The Jeremy Vine Show *on BBC Radio Two.*

Terry Waite

I HAVE VERY FOND MEMORIES of my grandmother. She was an accomplished pianist and whenever I visited her home (which was not too frequently as she lived quite a distance away) I would ask her to play for me.

During the time of the Great Depression, she eked out the family income by playing the piano for the silent films, and of course I always asked her to play her repertoire which she did with great gusto. She always wanted me to learn the piano but, alas, family resources did not extend to buying one. And to this day, it is one of my regrets that I never did learn. Perhaps retirement, when it eventually comes, will provide me with the opportunity!

> " **... she eked out the family income by playing the piano for the silent films ...** "

Former Special Envoy of the Archbishop of Canterbury, Terry Waite CBE was held hostage in Lebanon from January 1987 until November 1991. A great humanitarian, he is now a lecturer and writer.

Zoë Wanamaker

MY PATERNAL GRANDPARENTS were Russian peasant Jewish émigrés who settled in Chicago at the very young ages of eleven and twelve. They then moved in retirement to California.

On their first visit to England, they went to Stratford-upon-Avon and were shown Anne Hathaway's cottage and various other houses with thatched roofs. My grandmother, when asked whether she had enjoyed her tour, said: "Zees English are so poor. They have straw on their roofs. But we have tiles!"

My grandmother used to burp very loudly and never apologised for it but would just say "Oi, oi, my oesophagus!" She didn't know what it meant, but it seemed to work as an excuse.

> " **Zees English are so poor. They have straw on their roofs. But we have tiles!** "

The sadness is I really didn't know my grandparents because they lived in California and it was so expensive to visit them – or even to telephone them then – and so we never grew up with them. I missed that connection of having grandparents nearby. I think it teaches you respect and tolerance.

Zoë Wanamaker CBE has a distinguished stage career, as well as making frequent television appearances, and has recently been seen the world over playing Madam Hooch, the Quidditch teacher in the recent Harry Potter films.

Paul Weller

WITHOUT GETTING too deep about it, it makes me see the whole lifecycle and the whole continuation of life in a positive way. Even though we all perish, there is this continuum ....

The relationship between grandparents and grandchildren is very different to the one which exists between parents and children. They're like idealised versions of parents who, as far as the grandchildren are concerned, can do no wrong. That's what I get from it.

One of the things I really wish for is to be alive long enough not only to see my own children grow up but also to see their children grow up. To become a grandparent one day myself. I can see certain character traits have been passed down from my father John to myself, and then to my own children. The most obvious one is probably a certain grumpiness! I suppose the thing about tightly-knit families is that your kids have a good chance of growing up to be decent human beings. Nathaniel (my eldest) is fifteen – and he's not out shoplifting and smoking crack or anything, he's a really nice lad.

My son and my eldest daughter spend a lot of time with the grandparents the other two don't have. They all go on holiday once a year together to Sorrento, Italy. And it's been like that since they were weeny, since they were babies. Every couple of months they'll go down and spend a weekend with them. They get spoiled to death obviously, which is a grandparent's prerogative. All those things are attractive to kids, and they're not so "on their case" as either their Mum or I might be.

I think the relationship between grandchildren and grandparents is really important for society in general, definitely. And we're incredibly lucky if our parents are into our kids because there are an awful lot of people who aren't able to say that. It's important for the older generation to have some respect for the younger and for the younger generation to have some respect for the older. I know it's a cliché but it's true. Also for them to see there is some real ancestry, to recognise that they're not bang, on the planet one day and off it the next. That they haven't just come out of nowhere.

I definitely see it in my Dad who, as anyone who's met him knows, is a pretty cool customer. Watching him playing with the kids you see another really gentle side to him.

> " The relationship between grandparents and grandchildren is very different to the one which exists between parents and children. They're like idealised versions of parents who, as far as the grandchildren are concerned, can do no wrong. "

A singer, songwriter and musician, Paul Weller performed with The Jam and The Style Council, and in 1991 began his highly successful career as a solo artist.

Simon Weston

I HAVE many happy memories of my childhood: day trips to Bristol Zoo, sunny afternoons at Sandy Bay in Porthcawl.

There are one or two memories that cause me still to smile. One of the greatest influences on my young life has to be my grandfather (Gransha), Percy Swattridge. He was physically a small man, but he had the spirit and character of a giant. This is the man who, as poor as we were, created lampshades out of foil pie tins, who cooked a better dinner than my Gran (though she would never admit it) and most importantly he made us all laugh. With his jokes and his face pulling we would soon be falling about.

One of my last memories of this man was laughing at his months of effort to get our youngster to say his first word. The hours spent walking up and down, playing and encouraging this all-important step in the baby's development … and there it was the moment his mother and I had waited for …"bugger". As funny as that was at the time, it wasn't so funny, as we spent equally as long trying to discourage him from saying his first swear word!

Gransha was a typical Merthyr Tydfil Welshman, and my greatest sorrow is that my children never got the chance to know him as the wonderful man he was.

Simon Weston OBE was born in Wales in 1961. He has written and spoken with great courage about coming to terms with facial disfigurement and repeated surgery after injuries received while serving in the Falklands War.

Richard Whiteley

**MY MATERNAL GRANDPARENTS died when my
mother was a child, but I did have Grandpa and
Grandmother Whiteley.**

My grandmother died when I was six or seven, so I don't remember her
very well, but my Grandpa (Samuel Johnson Whiteley) came to live with us
when Granny died. We lived on the outskirts of a suburban village near
Bradford, yards from some fields and farms. We used to go walking down
to the farm together.

A particularly interesting point is his name – Samuel Johnson Whiteley. The
great Samuel Johnson was the man who compiled the first English
dictionary and without whom there would be no dictionaries, and therefore
no *Countdown*!

Grandpa was of the second generation of Whiteleys who ran a textile mill
in Bradford. Thomas Whiteley, my great-grandfather, was a typically bluff
Yorkshire textile mill owner. He was a prosperous man, who at one point
was president of The Halifax Permanent Benefit Building and Investment
Society which later became the Halifax Building Society (and is now HBOS
plc). I actually have his picture in my house now.

My grandfather had three brothers: Lewis, Percy and Frank, and two
sisters, Agnes and May. All of the sons worked in the mill.

Every day he would wear a suit, a waistcoat and a watch-chain. He was very
much a "gentleman of the old school". He would always keep notes about

observations and such things as what he had bought in the shops that day. He was a very benign, gentle and elegant man.

We share a number of the character traits. We are both hoarders, both sentimentalists and both share a love of Yorkshire. I always remember his birthday – August 5th.

I remember going to tea on Sunday afternoons at his house in Ilkley and eating potted meat sandwiches. Afterwards we would go for walks round town – the highlight being making echoes under the railway bridge.

He didn't really approve of or understand television. He preferred "spot the ball". There was a programme called *Saturday Special*, which I would watch religiously. A chap called Peter Butterworth presented it, so whatever was on, Grandpa would walk in the room and say gruffly: "Is this Butterworth?" This was incredibly annoying for an eight-year-old child!

Television personality Richard Whiteley OBE is best known as the presenter of Countdown.

June Whitfield

I owe a great deal to my maternal grandmother. She was a good needlewoman and made endless costumes for me when my dancing school put on its annual display at the then Brighton Empress.

Gran also took me to the cinema and to the great stars of the day – Judy Garland, Spencer Tracey and Katherine Hepburn, Glen Ford, Clark Gable, Astaire and Rogers – and we'd have fish and chips in the Astoria restaurant before or after the film. Thank you, Gran, great days.

One of the great treasures of British comedy, June Whitfield CBE has played a host of memorable character roles including Ethel in The Glumms, *June in* Terry and June, *and more recently, Edina's long-suffering mother in* Absolutely Fabulous.

Ann Widdecombe

I NEVER KNEW EITHER GRANDFATHER, but I knew my maternal grandmother very well, she lived with me throughout my childhood.

She, Florence Susan Plummer, came to live with us after she was bombed out during the Second World War and lost everything.

She arrived at my parent's home with very little more than what she was standing up in. This was in 1940. I was born in 1947, and she died when I was fourteen. I was devastated when she died because she was, in a sense, a second mother to me. It happened in December, while I was away at boarding school. We looked after her at home so she never went to hospital. It was shattering. We used to listen to the radio together. She taught me to read and do my times tables before I went to school. She sang to me and read all sorts of poetry to me, some of which I can remember to this day.

She was very kind, my grandmother. My mother always used to say that she would give away her heartstrings. She taught me to see beyond superficialities. I was always encouraged at home to have any children over to play in an age when they used to make the most excruciating class distinctions between officers' children and others. My grandmother and parents would have none of it. They said that everybody is equal before the sight of Almighty God. That could be where my meritocratic view of politics comes from.

Florence was a very religious woman, she taught me to say my prayers – which I did every night of my childhood. I think about her a lot – she was badly crippled with arthritis and in those days there were no hip replacements so nowadays I am always campaigning for my constituents to get hip replacements. I sometimes think that if my grandmother were alive today and she had been told that she could have a hip replacement in two years, but she would have to go to Inverness to get it, she would have thought a miracle was happening. Whereas now we want it in a month and we want it on our doorstep. This is all good and proper; however it does illustrate how aspirations have utterly changed.

My paternal grandmother, Alice Murray Widdecombe, rotated her time between her four children. She spent two months per year with us, so for those two months I had two grandmothers in the house, which was great.

I think that the grandparent-grandchild relationship is crucial firstly because it mixes the generations and secondly, from the point of view of shared experience. A lot of the things that go wrong are due to youngsters setting up independent homes at the age of twenty or twenty-one, and being deprived of the wisdom of previous generations. Very often, doctors complain about mothers calling them out for what they regard to be trivia. This is often because they do not have someone older there to tell them that this need not be something to worry about. Conversely a grandparent can tell you that there are things you should worry about if they have not seen or experienced them before. I believe this relationship to be imperative. I believe that families should be a large unit all caring for one another. My mother nursed her mother and my father. It was not something we questioned; it was something we regarded as completely natural.

The Rt Hon Ann Widdecombe is the Conservative MP for Maidstone and the Weald. She held several ministerial appointments in John Major's Government, and more recently has been Shadow Secretary of State for Health and Shadow Home Secretary. She also writes novels and appears regularly on radio and television.

Shaun Williamson

*The grandparent-grandchild relationship
is so precious because it gives
the grandparents a second and final crack
at witnessing the joys of childhood.
My Mother, Irene, is my four-year-old
daughter Sophie's best friend
and their relationship is a joy to behold.*

Actor, singer and comedian Shaun Williamson played Barry Evans in Eastenders. *He has recently
made his West End debut in the musical* Saturday Night Fever.

Terry Wogan

I NEVER KNEW MY PATERNAL GRANDPARENTS. My father's father drank the family business away, in the time-honoured Irish fashion, and my father had to serve his time as a grocer's curate.

My Dad loved his mother and hated his father, which is why, I suppose, he was such a loving, gentle father himself.

My recollections of my mother's parents are misty, when it comes to my Grandad. He was a Sergeant Major in the British Army. I have a picture of him at home, and he's the living spit of my brother if you can forget the waxed moustache. Actually, that moustache is the only thing I can remember about him.

He must have been a lovely man, though, because my Granny loved him, and she was the sweetest, gentlest creature that ever was born. Everybody called her Muds – not that she could hear them all that well. As long as I knew her, she wore a hearing-aid that was always tuned too low. Because when she turned it up, it whistled, and every dog in Dublin rushed to her side …. My Granny could cook, which is more than you could ever say about my Mother, who

> " As long as I knew her, she wore a hearing-aid that was always tuned too low. Because when she turned it up, it whistled, and every dog in Dublin rushed to her side …. "

freely admitted to being unable to boil water. I can only assume that my love of good food comes directly from Granny ….

> " … it's that much easier to give love if you've been lucky enough to receive it all your life. "

As to the rest, I have always regarded myself as the luckiest of men. Throughout my childhood, I knew nothing but love, and nothing of unhappiness, nor deprivation. It has been that way throughout my adult life as well. And it's that much easier to give love if you've been lucky enough to receive it all your life. I believe that it comes down through the generations, the greatest gift that grandparents and parents can bestow. When you get it, you pass it on, and on, and on ….

The smooth-talking radio and TV personality, with his Irish charm, needs no introduction. Terry Wogan OBE has been chatting his way into the hearts of the British public for nigh on forty years.

Personal Postscript

A Sequel?

THE COMPILERS OF 'FALSE TEETH AND A SMOKING MERMAID' are keen to produce a people's version.

If you have enjoyed reading the wonderful memories which contributors to this book have of their grandparents, you may be thinking that you too have some equally special memories of your grandparent or grandparents which you would like to share with the world.

For every celebrity who has so generously shared their memories in "False teeth and a smoking mermaid", we know there are thousands of other people who have equally special memories or stories about one or more of their grandparents.

If you remember your grandparents, why not see if your memories can make it into our proposed next collection? The idea of this sequel is to enable people from all walks of life to tell their stories, and the best will be selected for inclusion. Don't miss your chance to tell the world about your experience of this special relationship, and to immortalise your grandparents.

HOW TO SEND US YOUR STORY

Just go to www.ultimategrandparent.com and click on "False teeth and a smoking mermaid – the sequel" and see how to give us your story for inclusion. The Grimaldi family, whose great-great-grandfather Kaka was the inspiration for this book (see the introduction on pages 1–4), plans to compile the sequel over the next year. A selection of your stories will also be featured on the website. Guidelines for entry are available from www.ultimategrandparent.com

About Age Concern

THIS BOOK IS ONE of a wide range of publications produced by Age Concern England.

Age Concern is the UK's largest organisation working for and with older people to enable them to make more of life. We are a federation of over 400 independent charities which share the same name, values and standards.

We believe that ageing is a normal part of life, and that later life should be fulfilling, enjoyable and productive. We enable older people by providing services and grants, researching their needs and opinions, influencing government and media, and through other innovative and dynamic projects.

Every day we provide vital services, information and support to thousands of older people of all ages and backgrounds.

Age Concern also works with many older people from disadvantaged or marginalised groups such as those living in rural areas or black and minority ethnic elders.

Age Concern is dependent on donations, covenants and legacies.

Age Concern England
1268 London Road
London SW16 4ER
Tel: 020 8765 7200
Fax: 020 8765 7211
Website: www.ageconcern.org.uk

Age Concern Scotland
113 Rose Street
Edinburgh EH2 3DT
Tel: 0131 220 3345
Fax: 0131 220 2779
Website: www.ageconcernscotland.org.uk

Age Concern Cymru
4th Floor
1 Cathedral Road
Cardiff CF11 9SD
Tel: 029 2037 1566
Fax: 029 2039 9562
Website: www.accymru.org.uk

Age Concern Northern Ireland
3 Lower Crescent
Belfast BT7 1NR
Tel: 028 9024 5729
Fax: 028 9023 5497
Website: www.ageconcernni.org

Age Concern Books

Age Concern Books is pleased to offer a discount on orders totalling 50 or more copies of the same title. For details, please contact Age Concern Books on 0870 44 22 120.

Visit our website at: www.ageconcern.org.uk/shop

Age Concern Information Line/Factsheets subscription

Age Concern produces over 45 comprehensive factsheets designed to answer many of the questions older people (or those advising them) may have. These include money and benefits, health, community care, leisure and education, and housing. For up to five free factsheets, telephone: 0800 00 99 66 (7am–7pm, seven days a week, every week of the year). Alternatively you may prefer to write to Age Concern, FREEPOST (SWB 30375), ASHBURTON, Devon TQ13 7ZZ.

For professionals working with older people, the factsheets are available on an annual subscription service, which includes updates throughout the year. For further details and costs of the subscription, please write to Age Concern at the above Freepost address.

About Railway Children

The Railway Children charity works for the millions of street children in the world who leave their homes and first come into contact with the harsh realities of street life on the main railway and bus stations. Railway stations are often a magnet for these children. They arrive on trains, or they may head there hoping to find food and shelter. During the first few days, runaway children are particularly at risk and are often exploited by adults and older children.

The purpose of Railway Children is to make contact with these runaway, abandoned, abused and sick children as they arrive at railway stations around the world. We provide a caring point of contact for children coming onto the streets, giving help and advice and reuniting them with their families, if possible. We also provide shelter, healthcare, education, training, protection and, above all, friendship. We fund projects in the UK, India, Siberia, Russia and Mexico.

Contact us at:
Unit G8
Scope House,
Weston Road,
Crewe, Cheshire,
CW1 6DD

Telephone: 01270 251571
Email: enquiries@railwaychildren.org.uk
Website: www.railwaychildren.org.uk

Lynda Bellingham with her grandparents

*Cherie Booth, her mother, younger sister and
paternal grandparents, Vera and George*

*Stephanie Cook on the knee of her great-grandmother
with her sister Vanessa standing next to her great-
grandfather
Below, four generations of the Cook family with
Stephanie to Great-Grandpa's left*

Jilly Cooper's grandmother

Edwina Currie's grandparents

Tony Jardine's grandparents Tommy and Cath, and below, his Grandad Tommy as a naval engineer

Rose Gray with her grandmother

*Kathy Lette's grandmother
Mary Elsie Grieve at 100
years of age*

*Ellen MacArthur aged 8 with Gran and Nan and little
brother*

Ellen MacArthur's Nan's graduation day

Ellen MacArthur being greeted by Nan after her Round Britain Sail

Steve Pemberton's christening

David Owen on his grandfather's shoulders

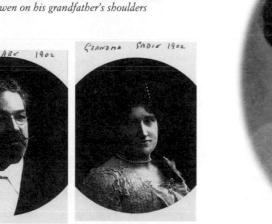

Stirling Moss' grandfather and grandmother

Angela Rippon's grandmother

Gift books for grandparents

Gardening In Retirement
Bernard Salt

This book is for both those who are actively looking for a challenge and those who experience difficulties with everyday tasks. It offers tips on making jobs easier, covers organic as well as conventional gardening, and is illustrated with over 300 colour photographs. Subjects covered include patios, lawns, trees, fruit and vegetables, safety, recycling, and care of wildlife and the environment.

£6.49 (RRP £12.99) 0-86242-311-2

Retiring To Spain: Everything You Need To Know
Cyril Holbrook

Once free of the shackles of earning a living, thousands of British people make the momentous move to head south to the sun – especially to Spain. Living abroad is an entirely different experience from going there on holiday. This book will help you avoid many of the pitfalls, and make the transition to a sunny and healthy retirement a reality. It contains chapters on the pros and cons of living abroad, where to settle, when to move, finances, property, town halls and taxes, monitoring matters, quality of life, pets and pastimes, healthcare, security, common complaints, and going home to the UK. The text contains many real life anecdotes and stories to illustrate the points made, as well as a list of useful contacts and addresses.

£7.99   0-86242-385-6

**Getting The Most From Your Computer: Second Edition
(including free CD-ROM)
A practical guide for older home users
Jackie Sherman**

Thoroughly revised and updated, the second edition of this bestselling title now includes the new Windows XP operating system, a free CD-ROM containing extra material, even more help for beginners, step-by-step instructions, exercises at the end of each chapter to help test your skills, full colour screen shots and illustrations, guidance for people with disabilities, and material on using scanners and digital cameras.

The text continues to offer essential background information for all computer users to enable them to take control of their lives, to stay in touch with family and friends, to meet new people or arrange holidays and leisure activities, and to order food or goods to be delivered at home. With its highly successful track record, this book is a "must" for anyone with an interest in computing and wanting to keep pace with all that computers have to offer in terms of daily living.

£7.99   0-86242-392-9   Available November 2005

How To Be A Silver Surfer: Second Edition
A beginner's guide to the Internet
Emma Aldridge

This revised edition of this hugely successful book contains new chapters on using the Internet for shopping, banking, tracing family trees and gardening. It is a companion guide for people who are new to the Internet, and a little apprehensive about how to use it. Using simple step-by-step explanations, the text guides readers through the most important tasks when using the Internet. Topics include searching the web, sending an e-mail, and saving a favourite web page for future reference. One of Age Concern's top-selling titles.

£5.99   0-86242-379-1

Know Your Complementary Therapies
Eileen Inge Herzberg

This title provides an introduction to a comprehensive range of complementary therapies including acupuncture, herbal medicine, aromatherapy, spiritual healing, homeopathy and osteopathy. Clearly written, it provides background information on each therapy covered, and also explains what they involve and how they work. The Useful Addresses section at the back of the book enables readers to contact the appropriate UK societies, associations and governing bodies for each therapy, should they wish to find out more about any of the therapies covered.

£9.99   0-86242-309-0

Personal memories of my grandparents

Personal memories of my grandparents

Personal memories of my grandparents

Personal memories of my grandparents